THE SMARTER STARTUP

A Better Approach to Online Business for Entrepeneurs

NEAL CABAGE & SONYA ZHANG, PhD

New Riders

VOICES THAT MATTER™

The Smarter Startup: A Better Approach to Online Business for Entrepreneurs
Neal Cabage and Sonya Zhang

New Riders
www.newriders.com

To report errors, please send a note to errata@peachpit.com

New Riders is an imprint of Peachpit, a division of Pearson Education.

Copyright © 2013 by Neal Cabage and Sonya Zhang

Project Editor: Michael J. Nolan
Production Editor: Danielle Foster
Development Editor: Margaret S. Anderson
Copyeditor: Gretchen Dykstra
Proofreader: Patricia Pane
Indexer: Joy Dean Lee
Cover & Interior Designer: Charlene Charles-Will and Danielle Foster
Compositor: Danielle Foster

ISBN 13: 978-0-321-90501-7
ISBN 10: 0-321-90501-6

9 8 7 6 5 4 3 2 1

Printed and bound in the United States of America

Dedicated to Kelly & Ethan.

ACKNOWLEDGEMENTS

This book was written for all of the entrepreneurs and "wannaprenuers," who are either working hard to build a business of their own or dream of someday doing so. We have learned so much from talking with the community over the years, reading blogs, watching interviews, and studying the successes. We hope this book will make a meaningful contribution back to the community, and to the conversation of how to build a successful startup.

Thanks to our families for their support during the writing of this book. Many hours went into research and writing, and we are grateful for their patience and understanding along the way. Thanks equally to our friends with whom we discussed our ideas and talked through our theories.

Thank you to everyone at New Riders, whose guidance was invaluable throughout the process of putting together this book: Michael Nolan for shepherding the process, Margaret Anderson, Gretchen Dykstra, and Patricia Pane for their careful attention to detail while editing the book, and Joy Dean Lee meticulously indexing the content. Charlene Will for her fantastic cover design, and Danielle Foster for her beautiful layout and persistence in overcoming the technical issues with our diagrams. Thanks to Glenn Bisignani and Laura Ross for coordinating marketing and outreach on behalf the book, and Lisa Matthews for her insight and advice on the college course material.

Please visit the official book website at:

http://TheSmarterStartup.com

CONTENTS AT A GLANCE

PART I
THINK

PART II
KNOW

PART III
DO

CONTENTS

PART I

THINK

PART II
KNOW

PART III

DO

INTRODUCTION

"Vision without action is daydreaming and action without vision is a nightmare."

You're probably reading this book because you're thinking about starting an online business or are already involved in one. And why not? In many respects, it is now easier to start a business than at any time in history, particularly an online business. The cost and complexity of launching a startup has fallen precipitously compared to even a decade ago. You no longer need an office, a phone system, or a climate-controlled server room. In many cases, you don't even need to write the core software your business will depend on—you can just plug into the cloud. And despite the lower cost of starting, finding capital to grow your business has never been easier.

Yet there are clear challenges that result from this new dynamic. Because it's so inexpensive to start a business online, a lot of people are doing it! In fact, if you've spent any time digging for that great unexploited online opportunity, you've likely already realized how difficult it is to find. And you're not just competing with other ambitious startups in your own backyard—you're up against every ambitious startup around the world. Some of these competitors have lower operating costs due to their geographic locations, while others are raising money from angels and venture capitalists, giving them tremendous leverage. Make no mistake, the Internet may represent the greatest boom in innovation-driven opportunity the world has ever known, but it comes with significant challenges, too.

The purpose of this book is to provide a conceptual framework for addressing these challenges. In the first section, we'll discuss the introspective aspects of finding and validating opportunities. In the second section, we'll focus on strategic alignment with external forces. And in the third section, we'll provide actionable advice for setting up your business, building your team, and developing your product offering. We'll walk you through the entire process, from making the first decision to become an entrepreneur to launching your first online business, and we'll tackle the significant strategic challenges.

Our goal in creating this book is to help startup entrepreneurs improve their odds of success and smooth the path along the way, conveying a deeper understanding of why some businesses succeed while others fail and how to deal with the challenges that arise along the way. We developed the book by compiling lessons learned from a decade of startup experience, studying some of the best practices in the industry, and balancing them with academic business models that help to clarify and provide depth. It is our sincere hope that this book will help you achieve your ultimate startup success.

—Neal Cabage and Sonya Zhang, PhD

PART I

THINK

CHAPTER 1

WHY BECOME AN ENTREPRENEUR?

"Success to me is not about money or status or fame, it's about finding a livelihood that brings me joy and self-sufficiency and a sense of contributing to the world."

—ANITA RODDICK

There are many reasons to become an entrepreneur and there's a good chance you've heard them before. We all know the stories of the boy geniuses who built billion-dollar companies in their garages after dropping out of college, or the social media startups that made their founders rich seemingly overnight. These are the rock stars of the new generation. They're doing things their way and having a significant impact on the world, and making substantial money along the way. Movies are even being made about them, telling their stories and glamorizing their journeys. Who wouldn't want to start an online business?

Alas, nothing is ever as simple or as great as it may first appear. Yes, entrepreneurship is an excellent way to control your own destiny and, for many, it's the best chance of becoming wealthy. But it's not without risk. For every Mark Zuckerberg or Steve Jobs, there are thousands of unknown entrepreneurs slogging it out in low-rent offices, working late nights and weekends, and stressing about whether they'll make payroll.

The odds of success are not high. A study by *Inc.* magazine and the National Business Incubator Association found the failure rate to be as high as 8 in 10 businesses.[1] Other studies agree that the odds of failure are higher than the odds of success but suggest the outlook is not quite so bleak. According to a 2005 study by the Bureau of Labor Statistics, "66 percent of new establishments were still in existence 2 years after their birth, and 44 percent were still in existence 4 years after."[2] As for Internet companies specifically, the report found that "despite the early success of the "dot-coms" during the 1990s, the information industry had the lowest 2- and 4-year survival rates, 63 percent and 38 percent, respectively". This is consistent with a 1989 study by Bruce Phillips and Bruce Kirchhoff who used the 1976–1986 United States Longitudinal Establishment Microdata (USLEM) compiled by the U.S. Small Business Administration and found that new establishments show an average survival rate of 39.8 percent after six years.

There are other challenges as well. If you're young, your decision to become an entrepreneur may be relatively simple, as you probably don't have to give up a promising career, worry about a mortgage, or feed a family. You are, however, most likely lacking savings to sustain you and, unless you were a particularly sharp study in college or from an entrepreneurial family, you probably have little knowledge of how to run a business, find product-market fit, or otherwise increase your odds of success!

Of course, there are positives, too. Most entrepreneurs cite personal freedom and control over their own destiny as primary motivators for starting a business. Others seek to change the world, or fall in love with the idea of shaping a company to match their own goals and values. There's also a certain dignity in not having to ask for time off to go to the doctor or attend an important family event. And who can ignore the allure of building a company that you can sell to fund your retirement at the end of your career.

---

1 http://www.inc.com/articles/201105/how-to-avoid-the-passion-trap.html

2 Bureau of Labor Statistics (2005), http://www.bls.gov/opub/mlr/2005/05/ressum.pdf

Clearly there are many pros and cons to becoming an entrepreneur, so it's not a decision to be taken lightly. The journey can be terrifically rewarding, but those rewards come at a cost and the path is riddled with pitfalls. The goal of this book is to help prepare you for the journey into entrepreneurship. We'll tear down the false assumptions of what it means to be a business owner, and build a better conceptual structure for what's required to find success along the way. Let's begin by taking a look within ourselves.

Follow your passion

Joe Penna once said, "Every single person I know who is successful at what they do is successful because they love doing it." It's easy to imagine why this is true, because without passion you're less likely to dig deeper than your competition or be content to work the long hours required to start a business. For this reason it's important to know your passion when deciding which of the world's problems you want to solve.

This isn't always a simple task. What about the boy who loves basketball but isn't tall enough to have career in the NBA—should he pursue a career as a professional basketball player? Should the girl who loves to sing but can't carry a tune become a professional musician? Clearly, it's important to possess talent, not just passion. Other issues emerge as well when you look more critically. For example, it's much more difficult to become a world-famous movie star if you have no opportunity to find your way to Hollywood and partake in the ritual of daily audition calls. So opportunity is also essential.

So how do you truly know if you should follow your passion? After researching this question extensively, the following criteria emerged as filters through which to measure the practicality of your passion: talent, reality, and audience (**Figure 1.1**).

Figure 1.1 Passion, talent, reality, audience.

Your talent

Everyone is naturally great at something. What's your talent? Think of something you enjoy, something that makes you lose track of time, something that makes you feel energized. Try thinking about it at an abstract level; don't try to pin down a specific activity. For example, if you're an artist, it might be the creative process that you love, not drawing per se. If you're attracted to sales, it could be that you're naturally social and enjoy making connections. If you can identify your talent in the abstract, you may realize that you have more options than you think you do, and one of these may coincide perfectly with opportunity.

Your reality

Unfortunately, not everyone has the same opportunities in life. Some are born with substantially more or fewer financial resources, while others have family or cultural constraints. The odds of finding success are much higher if you're realistic about these limitations and work to find solutions to remove them. For example, someone seeking to start the next great social network would face a significant burden if he tried to start such a company today. Catching up with the competition would require millions of dollars. Do you have access to the necessary capital, or are you realistically able to raise it? Are you willing to work long hours with limited income in the beginning while you launch this business? Having a family or family expectations may make this difficult.

Your audience

Perhaps the biggest problem with following your passion is that you can become supply driven rather than demand driven. In other words, you begin to think about what you *want* to do for a living, not what the world *needs* you to do. This can result in a misalignment of what you create or provide, compared to what the market will accept. Think instead about helping others and solving the problems you see in the world. By taking this approach, you will substantially increase the odds of finding a market for your product or service.

In short, nurture your passion, build your talent, negotiate with reality, and connect to your audience, and you will be more likely to succeed as an entrepreneur.

Will it make you happy?

Happiness is an important thing to consider. After all, most people discover entrepreneurship by seeking a better way compared to what they would otherwise be doing, and happiness is often the unspoken goal. For some, it's about freedom and autonomy. For others, it's about leaving a legacy or generating personal wealth. For still others, it's about social status and being the boss. But what happens if these goals are not met, or worse, you fall into a day-to-day existence that you don't actually enjoy?

Don't focus *solely* on outcome. What will your day-to-day existence be like? Is it compatible with the challenges and goals of your personal life? Is it aligned with who you are, your culture, and your goals outside of your career? These are equally significant things to consider when looking at entrepreneurship as a career. Starting a business requires a lot of work, it has a lot of ups and downs, and it can be stressful. Success is by no means guaranteed, so you really need to ask yourself if the path is a good fit for your personality. Are you up for the challenge? And are you the type that is likely to be successful in entrepreneurship?

What's your personality?

The field of psychology has produced an interesting body of research around the topic of personality and pairing it with career choices. Carl Jung first introduced the idea of psychological types in the 1920s.[3] Katherine Briggs and her daughter Isabel Briggs Myers later added to these ideas, creating the Myers-Briggs Type Indicator (MBTI), which assigns one of sixteen possible personalities based on a series of self-assessment questions (**Figure 1.2**). A generation later, in the 1950s, David Keirsey took up the task of applying MBTI and the related theories to determine appropriate societal roles and career choices. The resulting personality assessment test, known as the Keirsey Temperament Sorter,[4] is a common tool used by career counselors today.

When Jung first introduced the concept of personality types, he asserted that there were four fundamental types—two types and their opposites:

---

3 http://www.myersbriggs.org/my-mbti-personality-type/mbti-basics/isabel-briggs-myers.asp
4 http://en.wikipedia.org/wiki/Keirsey_Temperament_Sorter

introversion versus extroversion, and thinking versus feeling. Individuals were thought to be dominant in one of each of the two types; for example, one would be either more introverted or extroverted and more thinking or feeling. Thus one would combine the two types to determine one of eight possible combinations that describe his or her personality, such as introverted-thinking or extroverted-feeling.

Myers-Briggs expanded on this by adding two more dimensions: intuition versus sensing and judging versus perceiving (Figure 1.2). This resulted in a total of eight types and sixteen personality combinations. So, for example, a person's personality might be ENTP for example, indicating they are Extroverted, iNtuitive, Thinking, and Perceiving.

Guardians

- Supervisor (ESTJ)
- Inspector (ISTJ)
- Provider (ESFJ)
- Protector (ISFJ)

Artisans

- Promoter (ESTP)
- Crafter (ISTP)
- Performer (ESFP)
- Composer (ISFP)

Idealists

- Teacher (ENFJ)
- Counselor (INFJ)
- Champion (ENFP)
- Healer (INFP)

Rationals

- Field marshal (ENTJ)
- Mastermind (INTJ)
- Inventor (ENTP)
- Architect (INTP)

Figure 1.2
Myers-Briggs
personality types.

ATTITUDE: EXTROVERSION OR INTROVERSION (E/I)

People who are extroverted are considered "outward turning," whereas introverts are "inward turning." Extroverts are energized by action and social interactions, whereas introverts expend energy and feel drained by these activities. Some people are thus naturally good at activities such as sales, while others gravitate toward analysis and craftsmanship.

PERCEPTION FUNCTION: SENSING OR INTUITION (S/N)

How is external information perceived and understood? Sensing people tend to be literal and prefer facts and figures, whereas intuitive people naturally trust their gut instincts and subconscious thought. A classic analogy to describe this pair is that sensing people live and optimize well within the box, while the intuitive type spend their lives trying to reinvent the box.

JUDGING FUNCTION: THINKING OR FEELING (T/F)

Thinking versus feeling describes how one makes decisions using the information he or she has already perceived. In this regard, decision and perception go hand in hand as complementary functional types. The thinker is typically more logical in making decisions, using spreadsheets and analysis to come to a conclusion, whereas someone who is feeling dominant makes decisions based on emotion.

LIFESTYLE: JUDGING OR PERCEIVING (J/P)

Someone who is judging dominant focuses on making decisions with existing information, whereas someone who is perceiving dominant spends more time observing, listening, and collecting information. Notice that these functional types were described as perception and judging functions. Those who are judging tend to be more structural in their thoughts, while perceiving types tend to prefer less structure.

PUTTING IT TOGETHER

The combination of these types leads to sixteen possible personality combinations that describe a person's natural thought process. It is believed that by focusing on the way a person *thinks* rather than content of his or her thoughts, you can identify a personality type that will be stable throughout that person's lifetime. So while more content-oriented details such as your favorite television show or where you want to live may change along with age and emotional needs, your thought process and how you arrive at decisions will always be the same.

It is on this basis that Keirsey looked to provide a more actionable framework around observations by Jung, Myers, and Briggs. He ultimately concluded that the sixteen Myers-Briggs personality types were sound, though he placed more emphasis on the perceiving function than the judging function. He eventually profiled many prominent people throughout the United States whom he determined to be successful, and looked at these as optimal cases to determine career paths that were suitable for their personalities. Success is, after all, largely a function of having the right context in which your own strengths and weaknesses are optimal.

As a result of his additional research, Keirsey contributed the sixteen societal roles that can be attributed to the sixteen personality types first identified by Myers and Briggs.

Happiness and entrepreneurship

Now that we've explained personality theory, what does all of this have to do with whether entrepreneurship will make you happy? Consider the implications of these personality types and the answer to this question should be clear. Not every personality type would be ideally suited for entrepreneurship. And some may be compatible with entrepreneurship, but only in the context of a partnership to balance out their shortcomings, not as solo entrepreneurs.

It is generally agreed that ENTP and ENTJ are the ideal personality types for entrepreneurship. This type is well suited because their extroversion makes them outgoing and social, which is very important for business development and sales. Intuition is important for creativity and seeing what could be rather than what simply is. And their thinking approach to decision making makes them more rational and less prone to the emotional ups and downs of entrepreneurship.

The combination of these traits makes for the ideal entrepreneur. Keirsey identified the ENTJ type, in particular, as the field marshal role. This is a no-nonsense, action-oriented leader. This type would be excellent at leading a team in a business that depends more on execution than vision. The ENTP on the other hand is the innovator and thus more of a visionary. This type is equally able to motivate a team, but tends to rally the team toward innovation, not execution. An ENTJ (field marshal) might be ideal for a business with a sales focus, whereas the ENTP (inventor) might be more ideal for the technology startup in Silicon Valley, focused on developing an innovative product.

If you fall a little outside these ideals you may want to consider forming a partnership with someone who is opposite in that area. For example, the INTJ (mastermind) is an excellent analyst, strategist, and all around "product guy," but tends to shy away from business development and sales activities. For the INTP, spending a day making phone calls and pitching a product could be exhausting and unfulfilling. If you are an INTJ or INTP, look for a strong extrovert to carry those activities on your behalf or in partnership with you. Not only will he or she be better at this crucial activity, but you can focus on your strengths such as analysis and optimization.

If you're naturally a sensing type or feeling type, there's a good chance entrepreneurship is something you either happened into due to opportunity, or something you never fully considered as a career path, since the uncertainty and lack of security would be a challenge to your composition. But that doesn't mean these types are ill equipped for every type of entrepreneurship. In fact, sensing types would excel in certain professional services such as accounting or law and thus could consider building a business around these activities.

Have you ever noticed there are some activities that we're naturally attracted to and others that we tend to avoid? Some people love social interaction, while others prefer solitude and more technical pursuits. When we pursue those things we're naturally attracted to, we tend to feel energized and excited rather than exhausted. We also will tend to find these pursuits more satisfying in the long term and are more likely to succeed by following our own strengths and interests, and satisfying our own emotional needs. You must be careful to separate your underlying personality from your cultural and social values.

Think of personality as the algorithm by which your brain processes information, and culture and social values as the content that you've absorbed along the way. Your values change over time, but your thought algorithm does not. We often adopt the values of those around us, regardless of whether they're a good match for our own personality. And this is what often leads young professionals to choose the wrong career path, only to wander aimlessly in their twenties or thirties until they figure out what they were meant to do. It's possible that you have been attracted to entrepreneurship because it's been elevated in the media with talk about all the newly minted Silicon Valley millionaires, or perhaps your parents are business owners. But these are not necessarily good reasons to choose that path yourself, nor are they predictive of your own success or happiness.

If you haven't already, consider taking either the MBTI or the Keirsey Temperament Sorter[5] test. The tests are available online and rely on honest self-assessment in responding to a series of questions. The official tests take about an hour and can be found on the official websites for a fee.[6] Or you can find many free, abridged versions of these tests online that can also approximate your personality. Whichever test you may choose to take, having even a basic idea of your personality profile, your strengths and weaknesses, will go a long way toward helping you to determine if you will be happy as an entrepreneur.

Why are some people lucky?

Why are some people so much luckier than others? And is it something that can be learned? When looking at successful entrepreneurs, it's tempting to dismiss success and say they simply got lucky. But to leave it there is to dismiss the phenomenon without understanding it, which, as it turns out, is part of the problem.

Psychologist Richard Wiseman published a paper called "The Luck Factor,"[7] which explored the phenomenon of why some people are consistently luckier than others. In this study, a group of participants were asked to count the number of pictures in a newspaper. Some found the answer within a couple seconds while others took over two minutes. Why? It turns out there was a large advertisement on page two that read "Stop counting. The answer is 43. Tell the experimenter you have seen this and win $250." So, while some were hard at work counting the number of photos, others read this message, saw the opportunity, and stopped.

In a prior study by experimental psychologist Daniel Simons, a group of participants were asked to watch a video.

---

5 http://www.keirsey.com/products_overview.aspx

6 http://www.capt.org/take-mbti-assessment/mbti.htm

7 http://richardwiseman.files.wordpress.com/2011/09/the_luck_factor.pdf

In the video, participants are asked to count the number of times the team members with white shirts pass the basketball. In the middle of the video, a man in a gorilla suit walks in, stops, beats his chest, then slowly walks across the video. Once you know to look for it, it is incredibly obvious and hard to miss. But most do not see it the first time they watch the video. The effect is something called inattentional blindness.[8]

This would seem to suggest that most people get so caught up with solving problems in life or at work that their minds are too preoccupied to see the opportunities in front of them. But according to Wiseman, it's more than that. He identified four traits of the habitually lucky individual:

1. Observant of chance opportunity: As stated earlier, some people are not only more aware of opportunity, but also more open to those opportunities and seize on them as they arise.

2. Use of intuition to make decisions: Lucky people tend to follow intuition and trust that good things will occur by doing so. They don't get bogged down with spreadsheets and overly composed logical explanations.

3. Power of intention: According to *The Secret* by Rhonda Byrne, amazing things happen because we believe they will and we manifest them through the actions that come out of believing they will be. Wiseman talks about a similar effect. It's not just seeing the opportunity, it's having enough faith in your intuition enough to pursue it.

4. Resilience: Lucky people tend to handle bad luck much better than those who are less lucky. They tend to see how things could have been worse and feel grateful that it was not, rather than expecting perfection and shutting down when it is not achieved. This helps to keep the lucky person open to future opportunities and willing to follow their intuition next time.

The good news is that there's hope if you're not one of the lucky ones; according to Wiseman's research, you can train yourself to be more open and responsive to opportunity. Clearly though, some people are naturally better at this than others. And certain occupations train our thoughts against maintaining this mindset. Whereas a career in sales might provide daily interactions to remind you of the need to listen to and serve

---

8 http://en.wikipedia.org/wiki/Inattentional_blindness

those around you, a decade of intensive programming is likely to train your mind to focus on risk mitigation and avoidance, eliminating external and unforeseen variables.

These ideas are not isolated to an academic study. Religious writings from thousands of years ago tell us to develop our talents and to focus our efforts on helping others. Eastern philosophy meanwhile tells us to avoid attachments to the outcomes of our actions and states that the only way to know higher levels of consciousness is to be present in the moment, not distracted by thoughts about the past or future. Perhaps old-world wisdom is still true that we're most likely to find success if we listen to what others need from us and then focus on helping them with our talents. Is it possible that it's really just that simple?

Find your balance

Entrepreneurship can be fantastically rewarding, but beyond all the glamour there's a lot of work and sacrifice, and the majority of new companies that begin each year will not be around five years later—there are both high stakes and high rewards. This is why it's so important to know oneself before beginning on this path.

High-stakes opportunities may not be for everyone, but that doesn't mean you can't be an entrepreneur. Understand who you are. Be honest with yourself about your need for stability and predictability versus benefits such as being your own boss or creating an amazing new product. If you find that you require greater stability but still have the desire to be your own boss, consider starting a services firm rather than a high-flying software product. You may also want to consider aligning yourself with partners who balance your overall personality to improve your odds (**Figure 1.3**).

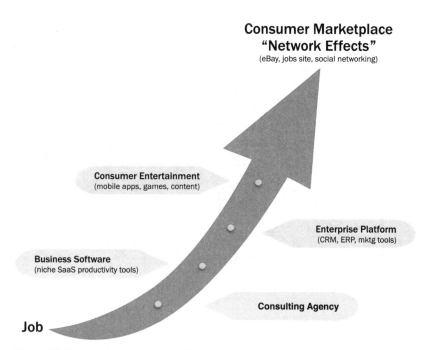

Figure 1.3 Increased reward comes with increased risk.

Try to be realistic and balance your passion with what the world will reward you for creating and your responsibilities in life. Your can combine these three prerogatives simply by thinking about how to solve problems for others rather than focusing on yourself. If you doubt that, consider the immortal words of Thomas Edison, who said, "I never perfected an invention that I did not think about in terms of the service it might give others . . . I find out what the world needs, then I proceed to invent."

By looking outside ourselves, we open ourselves up to hearing what the world wants from us; that, from the beginning, sets us on a trajectory for success.

Takeaways

- Passion is important, but so is a realistic assessment of your own talent, reality, and audience if you want to maximize your chances for success.

- The Myers-Briggs Type Indicator (MBTI) can help you understand your personality type, which can help you identify your strengths and weaknesses.

- Successful entrepreneurs are not simply lucky. They are more aware of opportunities, they use their intuition to make decisions, and they face failures positively.

CHAPTER 2

WHAT'S THE BIG IDEA?

"If people aren't telling you that your idea is crazy, then it is likely not a very big idea."

—FRANCIS FORD COPPOLLA

Not every business opportunity is equal. You can invest considerable time and money into an idea that you may personally believe in but which is not well aligned with demand, timing, or competitive forces. Despite your passion and commitment to the idea, if the conditions are not right, your efforts and investment could very likely be in vain. The opposite is also true. The Internet is rife with stories of small-time entrepreneurs who realized overnight success with very little investment of time or money.

How can we predict which opportunities are most likely to succeed prior to making significant commitments? In a fast-moving and dynamic market, it may not be possible to forecast with complete accuracy, but there are a number of accepted truths that may help us to at least approximate where best to put our efforts.

And so we begin this chapter. We'll start by providing a few thoughts that may be helpful for brainstorming ideas that you can build on. Then we'll introduce a framework we've developed to assist with validating and comparing opportunities, facilitating a more strategic approach to deciding which ideas are worth pursuing.

Brainstorming

Before jumping into the details let's define the foundational elements: Will you offer products or services? What market segment will you start with? And what industry will you serve?

PRODUCTS OR SERVICES

People from engineering or artisan backgrounds who have well-defined skills typically find themselves most interested in offering services. Services require less startup capital and often involve less up-front risk, so they're a good match for a small business. Conversely, many marketers or opportunity-driven business people are more attracted to products. Products cost a lot more to get started, often require startup capital and up-front risk, and typically involve more competition. But they also hold potential to scale far beyond what is possible with services. And once they're off the ground, they can often be more stable than services businesses. Some companies find a nice balance in between. For example, some consulting companies develop their own solution platform and provide customization and implementation services around their core platform product.

MARKET SEGMENT

What market segment will you serve: consumers, small businesses, mid-market, or enterprise? Consumers and small businesses rarely will pay for services unless they must (such as accounting or plumbing), but they have a strong appreciation for products. Any sort of service at this level needs to be template-based and packaged for efficiency. Conversely, enterprise businesses seek deep customization and will generally consider only products or services that will adapt to their own workflow and processes, not the other way around.

INDUSTRY

What industry do you want to serve? Some people are more opportunity oriented and may want to defer this question, but if you already have significant domain knowledge about a specific industry, that's a valuable asset to consider. If, for example, you were a real estate agent for five years, or worked in the insurance or entertainment industry, you may see opportunities that outsiders don't—if you decide to take a chance, your knowledge and professional connections may become the critical success factor. It's no secret that former employees of Apple, Google, Microsoft, or IBM have founded many great startups.

If you can answer the three questions above, then you've already substantially narrowed your scope and are ready to begin looking at ideas that you can plug into that box you've created. For example, if you've determined that you will create products for real estate agents (product, small business, real estate), then you've successfully created a box you can work within.

Evaluate what's out there

Before getting creative, take a few moments to identify businesses that are already providing products to the market you wish to address. As you go through this exercise, you'll become familiar with who's already out there, what they're providing, what seems crowded, and what is possibly even missing. Oftentimes, ideas come in the form of innovation, improving on something else you see or combining ideas or bridging gaps between existing offerings.

You may also begin to see patterns emerge; assuming you have chosen to focus on real estate agents, you may find that products for real estate agents cluster around four or five primary themes. That could be very useful information, both in terms of fitting the product model real estate agents have already formed and in finding ways to differentiate yourself from those clusters. So definitely take the time to research and understand who the players are and what products they're offering before trying to ideate too deeply. We'll discuss how to conduct market research to understand your competitors in the later chapters.

Solve a problem

As mentioned in Chapter 1, "Why Become an Entrepreneur?," one of the very best things entrepreneurs can do to improve the odds of success is to turn the focus away from themselves and instead look at how they can serve others. It is rare that someone has such a unique gift or such a powerful vision for the future that he is better off following his own inner voice than looking to help others.

Unless you have a strong conviction that you're the next Steve Jobs, it will most likely be in your best interest to look outside yourself. Focus on finding the pain points that others are experiencing and how you can help them. Is no one else helping them yet? Are there others with this problem? Can you bring scale and efficiency to solving this problem for others?

Look outside your sphere

Sometimes the best opportunities are found in places where others aren't looking. In an interview on Mixergy.com, Brian Crane suggested that entrepreneurs should "do things that aren't cool in California." This is a powerful idea. Consider that most software entrepreneurs either live in Silicon Valley or are culturally tied to it and the echo chamber of ideas that occur there.

Perhaps you're an entrepreneurial software engineer and you naturally gravitate to problems you can solve in things you know about, such as cloud computing, mobile apps, or Internet marketing. The problem is, every other person creating software is also of that culture and also focusing on cloud computing, mobile apps, and Internet marketing. This will, of course, lead to an excessive concentration of competitors around a relatively small set of ideas. Conversely, consider all the problems that software could solve outside Silicon Valley, and where uptake of technology may also be a bit delayed.

A rising tide lifts all boats

Have you ever noticed that people all seem to be interested in the same ideas for a while, then the fascination fades and everyone moves on to something new? It's as if the world's zeitgeist discovers and digests an idea collectively, no longer requiring it, once that problem has been solved.

In some cases these waves of interest are marketing driven and are merely fads that are gone as quickly as they come. But in other cases, they're a result of the market's absorption of something new, in which the wave of interest doesn't completely die off but rather settles to a more sustainable level after a little while.

Instances like these can present a significant opportunity for a new brand to enter a market since there are often no market leaders for this new market segment. As a result, the barriers to entry are low, considerable growth lies ahead, and thus returns can be much higher. Aligning your business with one of these waves of interest that follow the introduction of a new market segment can provide you with a clear advantage. Think about the explosion of new opportunities when the Internet was born. Smaller niches also exhibited similar waves, such as the advent of social media and mobile.

Think differently

Sometimes the best ideas come from simply approaching a well-defined solution a little bit differently. Apple did not invent the computer. Starbucks did not invent coffee. California Pizza Kitchen (CPK) did not invent pizza. Amazon didn't invent the e-book. Ikea did not invent furniture. Southwest did not invent airplanes. And Zappos did not invent shoes. Are you seeing a trend here?

Each of these companies has built wildly successful brands not by inventing a product, but by approaching things a little differently than the established competition. And by doing so, they created and thus dominated a new market segment. Apple, Starbucks, and CPK took a basic commodity and brought premium quality and features to it. Amazon and Ikea brought innovation to the distribution model that contributed significant incremental value. Southwest and Zappos brought exceptional customer service to industries that had commoditized to such a point that customer service was almost lost.

In each of these cases, brands found success by simply approaching their category differently and thus providing greater value to consumers. Sometimes the best opportunities are not even about creativity but rather about solving a problem for an existing industry and making it fun for consumers.

The role of innovation

Regarding innovation, Henry Ford once said, "If I had asked the public what they wanted, they would have said a faster horse." Media celebrates these innovators and thus we tend to believe that innovation is necessary for success in entrepreneurship, particularly with technology. Silicon

Valley is full of stories of daring entrepreneurs who followed their vision and changed the world. But is it true?

At first glance, innovation seems to be in the DNA of every major company that entrepreneurs emulate, but if we dig below the veneer it turns out not to be true. Most of today's Silicon Valley leaders were actually "fast followers," meaning they were the first follower that provided a well-executed iteration of someone else's innovation. For example, Apple was not the first personal computer developer. Facebook was not the first social network. Google was not the first search engine. In fact, when looking at successful companies in technology, this seems to be the rule—not the exception.

The value of pursuing innovation for young startups is that it keeps them tuned to early adopter-phase opportunities (we'll discuss this as part of timing in Chapter 5, "Competition and Positioning"). But that doesn't mean the best strategic position for a young startup is that of innovation leader. The risk and cost of taking on a research and development role early in the life of a young startup can be too much of a burden. For any startups, those resources would be better spent attempting to create a better user experience around a promising new idea that has already validated product-market fit, and capturing market share quickly.

Let the largest companies reinvest in technology through their research and development programs. If your technology startup succeeds, you, too, can be in a position to be an innovation leader later when it's better aligned with the status of your organization.

The power of the niche

It's very difficult for a new brand to enter an existing market and begin to compete directly with a market leader. Consider that the market leader already has a reputation and significant head start in marketing, so its conversion rates (conversions to sales) will be substantially better than yours. The leader has also already built up its systems and thus maintains a higher level of efficiency than a startup can. It may also have much larger cash reserves.

All of this means that the leader is much more likely to win any battle or challenge you may wage against, for territory it already occupies. You'd be much more likely to find success if you instead thought of a way around the market leader, rather than taking it on directly. Does it have a weakness you can attack? Is there a market segment it's ignoring? Are there near-market synergies it's ignoring?

The most obvious market niche opportunity, particularly for a young business, is to go after the premium version of a product or service. Because premium tends to be most service intensive, many large brands that have consolidated power around a product or service will eventually shed any services and focus instead on highly scaled, automated commodity production. That is precisely the opportunity that Apple and Starbucks seized on in their respective industries. Computers and coffee had become so commoditized that they lost any inspiration or joy they otherwise could have captured. That joy is what they brought back to these products, and it's precisely why they are so loved by consumers.

If the premium position is already occupied, another way to surface possible niches is to look at how you might combine two categories in the creation of a new category. For example, in Los Angeles a new shopping center phenomenon has emerged, which locals refer to as "shoppertainment." These are typically mega outdoor shopping centers that combine the utility of shopping with the experience of an amusement park. Universal CityWalk and Downtown Disney started by offering these sorts of complexes adjacent to their amusement parks in an effort to attract and retain visitors. Soon after, actual shopping centers started to adopt these ideas. The Grove in West Hollywood and Americana in Glendale look like movie sets, complete with Las Vegas-style water fountains that display dramatic choreographed water-to-music shows every hour.

Validate your idea

Hopefully by this point you've brainstormed a few ideas for your startup that you're ready to test. In this section, we'll discuss the Product Opportunity Evaluation Matrix (POEM) framework (**Figure 2.1**) that we've created to assist you in comparing the opportunities you've collected to determine which of these might be the strongest opportunity for you to invest in. While this framework is product-centric, the principles can be applied to services as well.

Figure 2.1 Peepholes into a black box, illustrating interpolation of data.

Imagine for a moment a large black box with several peepholes on the sides (Figure 2.1). You don't know what's inside, and looking through a single peephole gives you a partial view that isn't quite enough to make out what the object is. As you circle the box and look through more peepholes, you begin to get a clearer idea of what that object is.

This idea is similar to cell phone triangulation (**Figure 2.2**). Before GPS was ubiquitous on mobile devices, a cell phone's location could be approximated by querying three nearby cell phone towers. Each cell tower could provide only a non-directional radius distance from that tower. But by querying two additional towers and overlaying the distances as concentric circles, it was then possible to infer a general location where the device was located.

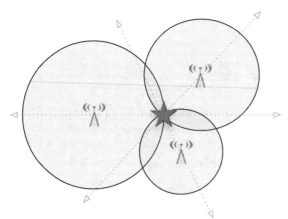

Figure 2.2 Cell phone tower triangulation.

We apply a similar approach to detecting where opportunity is for starting a business. It's not possible within a dynamic market to conclusively detect the location of a market opportunity, so we instead test opportunities against a set of accepted truisms that can demonstrate strength or surface weaknesses along an objective set of criteria. Using this framework, you can compare your ideas to see which is the most likely fit and may provide the most opportunity for your new startup.

The POEM framework comprises five filters that we pass ideas through. We assign a score to each filter and then evaluate ideas against one another based on their scores on the five filters. Each filter has five criteria that we call truisms, representing accepted truths about entrepreneurship that aren't necessarily scientifically validated or verifiable. Nonetheless, they provide a good set of criteria by which to judge an overall quality score for that particular filter (**Figure 2.3**).

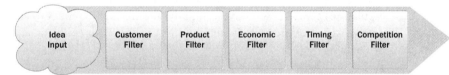

Figure 2.3 Product Opportunity Evaluation Matrix.

Customer filter

The first step should always be identifying a pain point that a would-be customer would pay to have solved. We must start by identifying a problem. If the problem is solved in a way that is meaningful to the consumer, she will reward the innovator financially. And so, all ideas must spring from this and be demand driven. Likewise, we must also identify clearly who the prospective customer is, how manageable the channel is, and whether the prospective customer has a desirable profile. Important criteria to consider here are:

1. Clearly identifiable customer

   The customer must be clearly identified and a persona should be created to represent this target customer. Scaling and optimization should be centered around understanding this client. Thus, a very clear and focused customer must be definable.

2. Meaningful problem to solve

   Is there an apparent and meaningful problem that this customer
   needs solved? If the problem is ambiguous, already has a solution
   on the market, or isn't significant enough to the client, consumers
   may not embrace your solution. A good question to ask prospective
   customers is, "What would you give up for this product or service?"

3. Segmentable market

   It's much more manageable to start with a small focus, achieve
   brand saturation, and perfect the model around a small niche, and
   then scale from there. Is the market something that can be sliced up
   horizontally to facilitate this approach?

4. Customer accessibility

   How accessible is the customer you wish to service? If you're
   attempting to serve an international market, tariffs and government
   regulations can be prohibitive. Similarly, attempting to market to an
   enterprise with bureaucracy surrounding procurement could also
   be challenging.

5. Customer loyalty

   Ideally, a customer is acquired then repeat business occurs thereafter, but this isn't always the case; some customer relationships are
   one-time transactions. This is particularly the case when catering to
   pass-through customers such as tourists. Is there an opportunity for
   repeat business or a longer-term relationship with this customer?
   What is the projected lifetime value of the prospective customer?

Product/Service filter

If the idea passes successfully through the customer filter, the next step is
to determine the validity of the product concept. Key criteria to consider
here are:

1. Tight niche focus

   The concept should be very clearly defined and narrowly focused,
   like a laser beam. If the initial idea is to be a comprehensive solution
   for someone, it's too broad. Instead, start with a core product and
   iterate the idea until it's validated in the market. Scale horizontally

to eventually create the comprehensive package for the identified demographic, as a growth strategy.

2. No network effect

   A business such as a social network or a marketplace grows in value exponentially as participants in that network grow. While this can be a potent multiplier, it's almost impossible to get off the ground without a significant budget. Thus, a Lean or "bootstrapped" business should stay away from any idea involving a network.

3. Lean method viable

   Lean methodology is a manufacturing process pioneered by the Toyota corporation that aims to solve the problem of discovering product market fit, rather than simply creating a product efficiently. Lean suggests marketing early and imperfect products rather than trying to get something perfect before taking it to market. This way, you can validate demand and profit margins before investing a lot of money in development. It also affords the opportunity to have users guide you to exactly what problem they need solved, and how to solve it. So, is your idea compatible with this methodology?

4. Team-to-product fit

   Not every team is capable of executing every idea. Does the team have the skills necessary to execute on the idea, or can such a team be easily assembled? This also has implications for competing effectively in the marketplace. Whether you'll be better off with a team of full-time, committed staff or a loosely organized group of contractors depends on the very nature of your business. Or you may start out being flexible and temporary and then, as your product or service matures, develop a team that's more stable and long-term.

5. Inherent story (virality)

   It's been said that good salesmen sell a story, not a product; if you don't have a story, you merely have a commodity and will eventually be competed into $0 margins. Thus it's important to determine whether the product concept lends itself well to a story that will engage prospective buyers. Is the product inherently viral, such that customers will want to tell their friends or colleagues? Both these things can have substantial impact on marketing costs, and hence profit margins.

Economic filter

The next step is to validate whether the financial aspects of the idea are viable. Are sufficient volume and margins possible? What sort of capital and cash flow are required to get off the ground? The criteria to consider here are:

1. Healthy margins

   Before investing time or money, it's critical to have a working model of how much it will cost to acquire a customer and service that customer, and what the profit tolerance of that customer might be, in order to model what the profit margins would be. What is the profit per unit of sale? How does this improve with efficiency of scale? Is it worth doing?

2. Demand constraints

   What is the total possible demand in the given marketplace? Is there sufficient potential demand that (along with margins) can justify going into business?

3. Supply constraints

   Are there limited resources that would affect your ability to service the customer? How will this affect the ability and cost of scaling up? For example, if you're in an agricultural or industrial town and require a large team of talented engineers, scaling might be an issue.

4. Sunk costs

   How much up-front money is required to get things started? Spending too much money up front is contrary to Lean methodology and represents a significant risk to the cash-strapped startup. Rather than spending a lot of money up front, it's best to use Lean to introduce an early-stage beta, validate the profit model, and get cash flow going, then gradually invest in the product over time. A healthy cost model designates a certain percent of revenue for product improvements over time. Otherwise, external funding is required. Remember, costs are always twice what is estimated, and revenues are likely half of what is estimated in the beginning.

5. Cash flow requirements

How much cash "float" is required for this business model? Some arbitrage models require a significant line of credit. Is that credit attainable? And at what cost? You'll need to account for these risks and costs.

Timing filter

Timing is often attributed to luck and other fuzzy things that can't be systematically accounted for it. This is unfortunate since timing seems to be one of the most important factors in predicting success. In fact, in the book *Blue Ocean Strategy,* Chan Kim asserts that studies by AT&T suggest that management teams, product, process, and other factors were all inferior predictors of success compared to simple timing. Moreover, he suggests that a company that's aligned with a larger, secular pattern that "lifts all boats" is more likely to succeed than a business that is not aligned with the larger, secular trend.

But what's the right time to jump on a trend? Companies have failed by being too early or too late to catch the wave, so to speak. To address this enigma, Everett Rogers introduced the Innovation Adoption Curve. We'll discuss this more deeply in Chapter 4, "Timing Is Everything," but the basic premise is to acknowledge a natural life cycle of any market, and to seek to enter early in that life cycle, before significant competition or critical mass has formed.

To address the timing filter, consider the following criteria:

1. Secular trend alignment

Is the idea aligned with a major secular pattern that will provide momentum? If not, you may spend a lot of money marketing a concept (and future competitors), not just your product.

2. Recent innovation enabler (early)

Is there some recent innovation or technology that suddenly makes the business model viable, where it wasn't just a few years ago? Some venture capital investors use this as a filter when evaluating businesses to invest in!

3. Market inefficiency (early)

   Is the market still inefficient? If you look at the stock market, it goes up and down quite a lot each day due to inefficiencies. These inefficiencies are caused by friction and ultimately represent opportunity. If the marketplace being considered is too efficient, it's already too controlled and the opportunities for a new entrant are small. It's better to find a Wild West scenario where the rules and systems don't yet exist.

4. Recent competition surge (late)

   If there are signs that a lot of people are rushing to the same place, it may indicate that the wave's early majority is currently building and hasn't crested just yet.

5. Signs of commoditization (late)

   If there are already signs of price competition tactics being used in the market, this indicates that the market is already late in the curve, and the opportunity window has closed. Keep in mind that technology is inherently a commodity.

Competition filter

If the idea passes through all the other filters, ask what the competitive landscape looks like. Is the market climate suitable for entry? Criteria to consider are:

1. Limited competition

   Is there a limited amount of competition? Is it possible to segment a way to really limit competition even further? Will there predictably be a lot of competition here quickly after you launch?

2. Competitor fitness

   How competent and sophisticated are the dominant competitors in your market segment? If they're getting away with offering substandard-quality products compared to a different market segment and are not reinvesting in their product to make it better, it may indicate complacency due to a lack of competition. This may signal a lethargic competitor that can be challenged with innovation.

3. Team fitness

   Not every team is capable of fighting a world-class competitor. Thus, it's important to assess who the competition currently is and who they will be in the future. Is your team capable of capturing and defending territory in this climate?

4. Defensible position

   Once a brand is established, is it possible to defend your territory, or are you vulnerable to price competition? Do you have a story or inherent differentiator that makes you uniquely qualified and your competition inferior?

5. Barriers to entry

   Are there important barriers to entry to acknowledge? Is there something that you'll trip on when you try to enter the market? Likewise, if you overcome this barrier, can it be used defensively to ensure less competition in the future? One benefit of an online software business (SaaS, or "software as a service") is that there's no barrier to entry and any engineer with a dream can put up an SaaS as a hobby, thus ensuring maximum competition.

Evaluate your idea

You can use the Product Opportunity Evaluation Matrix (POEM) chart shown in **Figure 2.4** to evaluate your startup idea across multiple criteria. There are two primary goals of this exercise: to expose any glaring weaknesses in your ideas by applying a standard set of questions, and to get a rough sense of which idea might be the strongest overall.

To use this framework, create a spreadsheet and populate the first criterion with the 25 criteria you must judge for each idea (five categories and five truism criteria per filter). Give each criterion a grade (A to F), then approximate a total grade for that filter group. After each group has a total grade, combine the group total grade to come up with one final grade. Think of this as a report card with an overall grade at the bottom.

Letter grades are used intentionally instead of numerical scores that would be easier to tally. This is because the framework isn't intended to be taken too literally, and letter grades intentionally obscure the sort of precision that might cause someone to take the results too literally. Keep in mind that the framework only approximates a complex and dynamic marketplace. Accuracy is also limited by the accuracy of one's own assessments and the scores given.

Despite these limitations, the framework can be a valuable tool in evaluating market opportunities by exposing important aspects of opportunities and imposing a structured and objective approach to evaluation.

i. Customer Filter		ii. Product/Service Filter	
• Clearly Identifiable Customer	[A-F]	• Tight Niche Focus	[ ]
• Meaningful Problem to Solve	[ ]	• No Network Effect	[ ]
• Segmentable market	[ ]	• Lean Method Viable	[ ]
• Customer Accessibility	[ ]	• Team-to-Market Fit	[ ]
• Customer Loyalty	[ ]	• Inherent Story (Virality)	[ ]
Overall Customer Score	___	**Overall Product Score**	___

iii. Economic Filter		iv. Timing Filter	
• Healthy Margins	[ ]	• Secular Trend Alignment	[ ]
• Demand Constraints	[ ]	• Recent Innovation Enabler	[ ]
• Supply Constraints	[ ]	• Market Inefficiency	[ ]
• Sunk Costs	[ ]	• Recent Competition Surge	[ ]
• Cash Flow Requirements	[ ]	• Signs of Commoditization	[ ]
Overall Financing Score	___	**Overall Timing Score**	___

v. Competition Filter		Overall Score	
• Limited Competition	[ ]	i. Customer Overall Score	[ ]
• Competitor Fitness	[ ]	ii. Product Overall Score	[ ]
• Team Fitness	[ ]	iii. Financing Overall Score	[ ]
• Defensible Position	[ ]	iv. Timing Overall Score	[ ]
• Barriers to Entry	[ ]	v. Competition Overall Score	[ ]
Overall Competition Score	___	**Total Overall Score**	___

Figure 2.4 Product Opportunity Evaluation Matrix (POEM) chart.

Make the decision

In his book *Brida*, Paulo Coelho wrote, "You must be careful never to allow doubt to paralyze you. Always take the decisions you need to take, even if you're not sure you're doing the right thing."

Coming up with the perfect idea for your business can be both tremendously fulfilling and exhausting. Inspiration and personal observations can form the basis of some of the best ideas, but don't rely on these alone, as there is a great body of knowledge available for predicting pain points, based on the experiences of those who've gone before you. The best approach relies on a balance of both deliberate and instinctual thought.

What's important at this point is simply to make sure your idea is reasonably well aligned with the opportunities that exist in the market, and that there are no significant flaws in your plans that are easy to identify before beginning. Don't sweat the small stuff. We'll talk about optimization and product/market-fit issues in later sections of this book.

Takeaways

- The best business opportunities come from looking for problems that need to be solved. Talk to prospects to understand how to address their needs.

- Discover areas of opportunity by looking at rising trends or talking to people outside of your own social sphere.

- Use the Product Opportunity Evaluation Matrix (POEM) to test your ideas and expose their shortcomings. The framework accounts for known challenges and will help you compare and choose the strongest idea.

CHAPTER 3

DO YOUR RESEARCH

"If we knew what it was we were doing,
it would not be called research, would it?"

—ALBERT EINSTEIN

Many entrepreneurs are instinctively doers and may not be inclined to postpone action in favor of things like market research. Ironically, taking the time to understand the market and its opportunities now can save you a lot of time and money later. More importantly, it can expose key data points that may affect your decisions on how or even whether to proceed. It's the classic argument to take the time up front to understand what you're doing before you begin.

With a little research you can expedite the effort of finding product-market fit, and reduce the time and money spent iterating on product ideas. And with competitive research, you'll be a lot better informed about who your competitors are, what their strengths and weaknesses are, what niches are perhaps saturated, and where the opportunities are perhaps ignored by your competitors. With this collective knowledge, you'll be in a much stronger position to make maximum use of your time and money.

Talk to your prospects

If you've found a market niche that you're interested in pursuing, talk to as many prospective customers as you can. Start by identifying who your typical prospect would be and reach out to as many people who fit that profile as you can. In the beginning you may simply want to have casual conversations with your prospects; take them to lunch and discuss their industry, their pains, and ask them what they think about your idea. It's possible you may get constructive feedback this way or perhaps even an unexpected idea or insight that sends you in a different direction.

Once you've determined that there's a demand for your idea and existing competition is not meeting your prospects' needs, consider formalizing your efforts a bit and reach out to even more people. Create a survey and ask each of your existing prospects to put you in touch with 10 contacts who could fill out a simple questionnaire to better inform your efforts. You can offer a free coffee voucher or free beta account in return. This can give you a more statistically significant sample that you can use for greater confidence or perhaps even to validate assumptions and decisions if you choose to raise capital later.

Having this early contact with your prospects is critical, particularly if you don't already have domain knowledge and a network within the industry. These connections will provide the eyes and ears you need for a better organic understanding of the problems your prospects face and the solutions they seek. You may even consider asking a couple of your better interviewees to become your advisors later when you build the team.

Test marketing

One of the most difficult aspects of entrepreneurship is finding product-market fit (the product, or service, that the market will be willing to pay for). Steve Blank[1] and Eric Ries[2] have famously advocated Lean methodology to assist young startups in accomplishing this challenge. Lean is a

---

1   Steve Blank (2005), *Four Steps to the Epiphany: Successful Strategies for Products that Win* CafePress.com

2   Eric Ries (2011), *The Lean Startup: How Today's Entrepreneurs Use Continuous Innovation to Create Radically Successful Businesses* Crown Publishing Group

methodology centered on user-feedback loops and just-in-time manufacturing. Toyota Motors has successfully applied Lean to more quickly find product-market fit and to optimize new feature sets before committing significant resources to full-scale manufacturing. Consider applying this same methodology to market research to validate ideas and opportunities.

There are many different approaches to test marketing. If you have a physical product, try listing it on eBay to discover its market value and demand. If you're offering an online service and you see a competitor that has an affiliate marketing program, you can sign up for the program and test market their product to see how it does.

Think also about marketing "vaporware" products via pay-per-click (PPC) advertising. Before spending money on product development, create a simple sales website for an online service you're considering. Select a website design that's typical of the type of product you might launch (probably Web 2.0 design). Provide the usual marketing copy and photos—make them professional enough that someone might actually sign up. Then create a sign-up sequence that lets customers register for the free version of the site.

If you want to better measure product viability and customer acquisition costs, you could offer a paid version only to determine how many people would sign up. For reasons of ethics and liability, you don't want to collect financial or even contact information using this approach, so you could just send them to a "coming soon" page once they've clicked the button to sign up. This would provide valuable information as to how easily you may be able to drive sign-ups.

This isn't a perfect test, of course. The numbers you get from an experiment like this will be lower than true sign-ups if your product had a reputation in the marketplace. Cost per click on these test ad campaigns will invariably be higher than long-term optimized campaigns, too. And let's not forget that you need to drive a statistically significant number of visitors to the site to have any meaningful data. The test also won't tell you how well other marketing channels might do compared to paid search only.

Despite its many flaws, this is one of the best ways to gain early insight into interest in your product idea. The data you collect won't be terribly meaningful in absolute terms, but it could be highly valuable relative to other product tests you might conduct, provided other variables remain constant, such as site design, marketing budgets, and so forth.

The real value of running these sorts of early test-marketing campaigns is the opportunity to quickly and affordably test several product concepts and iterations before building any actual functionality. Since the goals of Lean development are sound, applying the same principles to market research accelerates the process and reduces cost later.

Define your customer

In his 1998 book *The Inmates Are Running the Asylum,*[3] Alan Cooper described a method of formalizing customer research called personas. The idea is simple, but the benefits are profound. The persona provides a conceptual framework for defining a fictitious customer who represents the collective information you've gathered about your target market; creating a persona helps you understand user patterns before developing a product in response to your customers. The concept has become a core aspect of user-centered design and a common fixture in marketing as well.

Creating a persona starts with defining key attributes that reflect your typical customer, such as gender, age, marital status, location, education, occupation, income, and interests (**Figure 3.1**). With all this information in place, give the fictitious person a name and find a photograph that helps personalize the individual you've created.

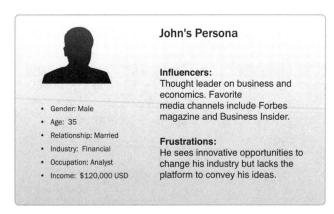

John's Persona

- Gender: Male
- Age: 35
- Relationship: Married
- Industry: Financial
- Occupation: Analyst
- Income: $120,000 USD

Influencers:
Thought leader on business and economics. Favorite media channels include Forbes magazine and Business Insider.

Frustrations:
He sees innovative opportunities to change his industry but lacks the platform to convey his ideas.

Figure 3.1
Example persona.

---

3 Alan Cooper (2004), *The Inmates Are Running the Asylum: Why High Tech Products Drive Us Crazy and How to Restore the Sanity* SAMs - Pearson

To add depth to your understanding, create a user story for your persona. The individual you've defined might be a 31-year-old real estate agent named Tom, but that's not necessarily the full story. If you're selling online marketing solutions for real estate agents, your first assumption might be that Tom is a prospective customer who is likely to buy. Subsequent customer research, however, may indicate that only independent agents make such purchases directly and that the majority of purchases are made by brokers representing their offices. So Tom might be a purchaser or quite possibly just an influencer who is researching options on behalf of the brokerage. This would be important information to consider.

The persona can be extremely helpful in ensuring that you've accounted for nuance and properly identified who your actual customer is. It's also useful from the perspective of communicating your findings across your team, and to reference later, when you're deep in product marketing and need a point of reference about who you're serving, what problem you're solving, and how best to communicate that solution to your audience.

Look at your competition

When beginning online marketing initiatives, sometimes you need to better understand the competitive landscape you're entering. It would be helpful to know who your competitors are, how they rank in terms of online visibility and income, how big they are, and which marketing channels they utilize. Competition being what it is, however, this information isn't always easy to come by. Fortunately, there's a lot of information to be found through various resources, if you know where to look. One of the goals in this chapter is to share methods figured out along the way.

Exposing key terms

The ideal first step would be to use a tool such as Google Keyword Tool, Wordtracker, or Keyword Discovery to identify the primary "head terms" for your specific vertical. By head terms, we mean the 10 percent of key phrases that get 90 percent of traffic. Each of these tools also provides a competition metric that can be useful. At the time of this writing, we prefer Wordtracker and a useful keyword indicator called Keyword Effectiveness Index (KEI), which compares total search volume with the total number of search results for a keyword. Google's Keyword Tool (part of AdWords) provides an analogous Competition score (low to medium) for each phrase.

For this exercise, we'll start by filtering key phrases based on volume, and then further refine until we find the top 10 key phrases. Note these along with the KEI index (or Competition score) provided by your keyword research tool (**Table 3.1**).

Table 3.1 Keyword Effectiveness Index (KEI)

KEYPHRASE	COMPETITION	SEARCHES	KEI
WordPress Themes	Medium	2,740,000	A
Educational Games	Medium	673,000	B
Software Reviews	Medium	450,000	B
Shopping Cart	High	1,000,000	C
Accounting Software	High	550,000	C
Website optimization	High	74,000	D
Real Estate Websites	High	110,000	D
Project Management Software	High	246,000	D
Property Management Software	High	40,500	D
Online Marketing Software	High	3,600	D

Surfacing competitors

Next, we'll search online for useful keywords that we validated, noting all the competitors we can find. Depending how deep we want to go, we can consider how many to take note of. To demonstrate, we noted around 50 competitors, with a goal of ultimately filtering them into four buckets, tier one to four, reflecting their level of competition. We use a spreadsheet to track all the various metrics compiled for each company we find. Let's now discuss what some of those metrics might be that we would want to track and compare.

Search engine results

One possible predictor of a popular or well-established company is how well it ranks in the search results. Google in particular has begun showing bias toward large or long-established brands, and its inbound link relevancy algorithm naturally favors large brands as well. So take note of how someone ranked for the top terms and assign him an overall grade of A to F. Take particular note of how well it ranks on the high KEI index (competitive) terms. You can also use sites such as OpenSiteExplorer.org to expose more quantified data such as MozRank and domain rank, which can be useful. Google's PageRank is also very useful as a separate metric. PageRank provides a 1 to 10 ranking of how substantial the inbound linking profile is for a given page and can be easily seen by installing the Quirk SearchStatus extension for Firefox.

Competitive ranking tools

Some tools that are particularly useful for this exercise attempt to track historic traffic for sites. Compete.com provides the last year of data for free (or two years for paid members) and allows you to compare up to five competitors on a multiline graph, to see who's truly getting traffic. Alexa.com provides a similar service and historic graphing but goes an additional step of providing a ranking number for each site; #1 is the most popular site on the Internet, whereas #100,000 is considerably less popular (**Figure 3.2**). Both of these tools work in part by providing a toolbar that users can install on their browsers to get extended functionality and data while surfing. In exchange, these companies get a sample set of data from which they can extrapolate general behaviors.

It's worth noting, however, that due to the nature of data collection, these sources (Alexa in particular) can tend to skew toward demographics that would be more male and early technology adopters. Assuming you're simply comparing businesses within a specific niche, however, this shouldn't be much of an issue. Quantcast.com is another tool of similar means (different data collection means) that can be used. We generally recommend getting data from all three of these to increase the overall reliability of your study. If you can triangulate a rough idea between the three, however, you'll be more assured of an accurate result.

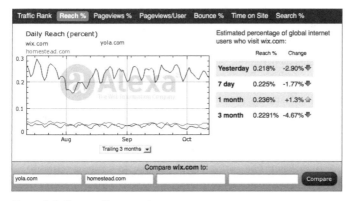

Figure 3.2 Alexa traffic comparison.

Alexa traffic approximation

The following chart shows a rough approximation of how Alexa rankings correspond to actual site traffic (**Figure 3.3**). There are, of course, outliers, but this is a good rough measure. We recommend tracking this as a separate metric.

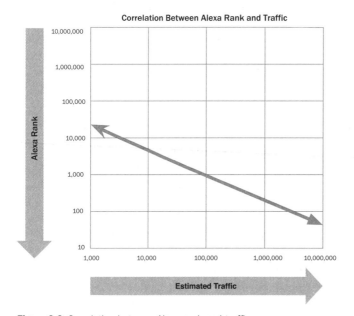

Figure 3.3 Correlation between Alexa rank and traffic.

AdWords spend

Are your competitors spending money on AdWords? Depending which vertical you're in, this could be more or less significant. If you're in business-to-consumer e-retail, however, this could be substantial. Amazing tools have emerged in recent years that can infer and approximate how well someone is doing on AdWords and what their estimated daily spend is. So, if PPC is a viable marketing channel, this can be a very strong indicator of how well your competitors are doing. As for specific tools, our favorite has been KeywordSpy.com, which crawls Google SERPs (Search Engine Results Page) and notes the PPC ads shown. The more frequently the ads appear as the bot crawls for that keyword, and the higher the ad position is each time, the higher the relative ranking that brand gets for that keyword. KeywordSpy then compares that to the keyword bid data to infer roughly how much money someone is paying per click, and collectively, their total daily spend. They also infer how well someone might be doing in terms of return on investment by looking at how consistently that brand has been present in their crawls. Someone who consistently ranks for a specific keyword must presumably be doing well. Pretty clever, huh?

Social presence

Another interesting metric can be found by looking at how well the company is represented socially. SEOMoz.org provides an excellent tool for assessing social mentions on the important channels, but requires a paid subscription to access that data. Klout.com also has a rather interesting and more in-depth way of assessing a brand's social value, and each brand is thus assigned a 1 to 100 Klout score. Radian6.com and a host of enterprise social monitoring tools further enable in-depth tracking and word counting for a high-level understanding of what the social activity is saying, not just that it exists.

Affiliate marketing

Many brands have an affiliate program, enabling independent agents or resellers to earn commission by directing sales to the brand. If a company has an affiliate program, it may be an indication of a more mature or established online brand. More importantly, it can signal that marketing channels will be congested with affiliates and cost of customer acquisition will be high due to the competition.

There's an upside to the existence of an affiliate program too, though. If you sign up and drive a little traffic, you can begin to see how well their products sell, what customer acquisition costs are, and so forth. If you're getting a 20 percent commission split as an affiliate, just multiply by five times to see exactly what their revenues are, and you can basically reverse engineer the entire cost and profit model of the business!

Business intelligence

Finally, there are two resources that are particularly useful for fleshing out a real-world business profile. Jigsaw.com is a crowd-sourced information directory owned by Salesforce.com. Jigsaw will tell you not only the business contact information, but also total employees, directors, sales of the company, and estimated revenue. Sometimes these ranges are a little too broad to be useful, but they provide a good base to start from.

Next, look for quarterly filings for any of these companies that happen to be public. You can get very precise data on head count, profits, losses, and margins, if so. In our experience, however, the companies we've profiled are rarely already public. More likely, you'll be profiling younger companies in up-and-coming sectors, in which case a couple are likely to have been recently profiled by Inc. 5000. If so, they'll tell you exactly how much revenue the company made and how many employees it has. CrunchBase.com is another useful tool for determining if any of these companies have raised funding along the way, and how much.

By compiling base ranges from Jigsaw and hopefully filling in exact numbers on 10 to 20 percent of your companies via other means, as well as compiling all the above data, you should be able to extrapolate approximately what the revenues, costs, and size are for nearly every business on your spreadsheet. And now you know who's who and can split them into tiers. Based on your own resources and history, you know which tier you belong in and are targeting. You now know precisely who your competitors are.

Here are the competitive analysis tools to consider for this exercise:

1. KeywordSpy.com

   This tool is primarily used for PPC campaign spying. You can see who's spending money on which keywords, and they'll roll this data up to give you an approximation of how much their daily total ad spend is. They also have a tab that shows competition for those key terms. This can be useful (in addition to simple Google searches) for identifying who the primary competitors are in a space.

2. Compete.com

   This tool approximates traffic for a website and provides one to two years of backward data, so you can see its traffic trends. Traffic estimates aren't terribly accurate, but they can be used in a relevant context.

3. Alexa.com

   This tool provides a ranking of how popular a site is. For example, Google may be number one, whereas your blog may be one millionth. Similar to Compete.com, its data accuracy is flawed but can be useful for relative comparisons.

4. SpyOnWeb.com

   Use this tool to see other sites that share the same Google Analytics to Google AdSense IDs. This can be useful for exposing competitors' site networks. A newer and similar tool is Blekko.com, though SpyOnWeb has been our favorite.

5. Chrome SEO

   This free plug-in for Chrome provides a convenient view of all the competitive metrics (such as Alexa, Compete, and PageRank) in one place, as well as backlink reports. This can be pretty useful and time-saving when compiling a competitive analysis spreadsheet of all this data.

6. Jigsaw.com

This crowd-sourced business directory from Salesforce.com is useful for approximating a company's revenue and staff size. The data is a broad estimation and should be used only if exact numbers aren't available from public quarterly reports, Inc. 5000, or press releases, but in the absence of those sources, it provides a good fallback.

7. Klout.com

This tool has introduced a composite index score that reflects your influence online, and thus can be used to determine how active and effective a competitor is on social media. Think of it like an Alexa ranking for social.

8. CrunchBase.com

This tool is a good way to validate whether a business has raised significant funds from angels or venture capitalists. The site is an offshoot of TechCrunch and keeps track of all of the funding activity in Internet-related businesses. Needless to say, when you're thinking about competing with someone, it's good information to know they just raised $100 million (that you don't have)!

Survey the battlefield

Having taken a look at the tools available, it should be clear how to roughly approximate the competition. The next step is to apply this across a large number of competitors online to better understand who your competition is, how they stack up, and equally, to better understand who the suppliers, prospective customers, and possible partners are.

If you're serious about entering a market, try to identify as many of the significant brands in your chosen market as you can. Create a spreadsheet of these vendors and use the competitive analysis tools discussed in the previous section to better understand how they rank. Important attributes to track for each brand might include:

* Product/service: What is their primary market offering?

* Pricing: What is their pricing model?

* Position: What niche within your vertical do they service? Are they up- or downmarket?

* Audience: What target market consumes their product or service?

* Location: What city are they located in? Are they local to you?

* Year founded: What year were they founded?

* Funding: What kind of initial or recent funding have they have raised?

* Google page rank: Google's page rank can tell if it's a significant online competitor.

* Alexa rank: Alexa rank can help to reaffirm Google's page rank. Neither alone is very accurate.

* Affiliate program: If there's an affiliate program, it can indicate a saturated online niche.

Once you've collected this data, you may begin to see patterns emerge. You'll begin to see well-defined subniches that all vendors tend to neatly fall within. You'll also begin to see who the leaders of each niche are, and which niches seem saturated compared to others. This information can be tremendously helpful in terms of identifying positioning opportunities for your new online product or service.

If you're a visual person, consider creating a diagram from this information after completing the analysis. A visual ecosystem diagram that illustrates relationships of subniches within your chosen market can serve as an excellent resource later, as you work on your marketing efforts.

Figure 3.4 illustrates the ecosystem of the real estate market. The diagram includes a few top competitors that were identified for each of these verticals, using the analysis described above, which profiled 170 competitors in the real estate market. It further shows how the niches build on or feed/inform other niches.

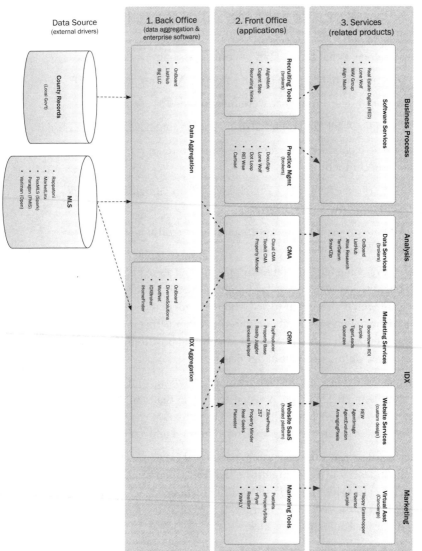

Figure 3.4 Realty ecosystem.

Pay attention to the 800-pound gorilla

Unless you're in a relatively new market, there's a good chance you have one or two public companies close by. These companies may seem tangential or irrelevant to your particular vertical, but watch out. They can move quickly through new product launch or competitor acquisition to consolidate a market and can put you in a bad position if you're not already occupying a solid, defensible position when it happens.

As a recent example, consider Seattle-based Zillow.com. Zillow raised nearly $90 million in private equity from 2007 to 2011 and finally went public in 2011 at a valuation of $539 million.[4] From 2007 to 2011, it aggressively built itself up as a leading search portal for real estate online. If you were an entrepreneur in the space you would be forgiven for assuming that was Zillow's charter and you had nothing to fear so long as you stayed out of the consumer search space.

In late 2011, however, the company bought DiverseSolutions,[5] which provides technology solutions for real estate agents looking to provide house listings on their own websites. At first blush, it was a curious but innocent move. In the months that followed, however, Zillow launched a free CRM (Customer Relationship Management) system, online training, free WordPress-based websites, and training videos for real estate agents looking to expand their online presence. A press release later stated Zillow's goals of becoming the online marketing destination for real estate agents.

The particularly surprising part of all of this is that the company offered all these services for free. It launched a freemium platform with hopes of upselling a percentage of its free traffic as a result,[6] and proceeded to hire a new team of 80 people, which appears to be primarily a sales team to push these new services to the market.[7]

---

4 http://www.crunchbase.com/company/zillow

5 http://www.inc.com/news/articles/201111/zillow-acquires-diverse-solutions.html

6 http://articles.businessinsider.com/2012-04-26/
   tech/31407871_1_zestimate-real-estate-agents/2

7 http://www.ocregister.com/articles/new-349482-zillow-hire.html

While this move provided significant new value for real estate agents, consider it from the perspective of the more than 100 small firms that provide online marketing and website services to real estate agents; Zillow effectively released a free version of products and services that the existing vendors were selling for $50 to $100 per month. Zillow's goal may have been to create a loss-leader freemium service to quickly onboard new clients for their new services offering, but by offering this loss-leader product for free, they effectively commoditized an entire industry overnight. This in turn put substantial downward pressure on prices and likely will lead to more than a few small businesses closing their doors over the next year.

The Zillow story is not an isolated one. Google has started to aggressively roll out free services in an effort to lure small businesses onto their platform and get them started with AdWords. Imagine if you had started a company specializing in small business websites and online advertising solutions. Only a couple of years ago, Google was a consumer-facing search engine. How did it become a low-cost, online marketing services company? Today it offers free websites, a free domain name, a simplified platform for small businesses to get started with AdWords, and online marketing reports and dashboards to help business better understand online marketing results and manage their online presence (**Figure 3.5**).

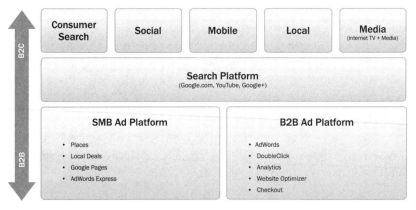

Figure 3.5 Google's product map.

That is not Google's only tangential free product offering. As of today, Google offers a high-quality analytics program, a social platform, a local deals platform, a mobile operating system, and payment transaction for ecommerce. It's working on cars that drive themselves, and it appears to be working on technology for a future Internet TV initiative. It offers all of this for free in an effort to control the search and online advertising ecosystem. This helps secure the company's future, establish relationships, and convert more businesses into paying advertisers for its primary consumer-facing search brand.

Amazon.com is the world's largest retailer. But in recent years it's also become one of the leading cloud platform service providers with its EC2 product. The move to EC2 at first seemed curious, but was followed by a hosted platform for businesses that want an online store but don't want to manage their own technology. And while EC2 is offered at reasonable utility hosting rates, the ecommerce platform is actually free for two years.

All these examples follow the same basic model, which is growing from consumer-facing brands to business-to-business (B2B) services and offering those services at significantly discounted cost. This acts as a loss leader to pull customers in, subsidizes operating cost by allowing B2B customers to subsidize those costs, plus provide the added benefit (to them) of driving out competition in the process.

While you may feel safe as a small business having found a differentiated segment or market niche, these are examples of why you still might not be protected if one of these large companies decides to offer your product or services for as a loss leader (for free). The net effect of their effort is to marginalize your business and drive the value of your product or services to zero.

The point is *not* to dissuade you from starting a company if there's a large competitor nearby, but to illustrate how important it is to identify these companies in your market and to understand their plans and look for warning signs that you might be in their crosshairs before you begin. If you can already identify an 800-pound gorilla in your target market, think defensively about this from day one. Think about how can you protect or differentiate against surprise attacks in the future, and build that into your business. Think also about how you can position your efforts out of harm's way if you anticipate the possibility of such a competitor entering your market.

Takeaways

- Market research is critical for calibrating your efforts with opportunity and competition you may not otherwise know about.

- Perform your marketing research from three perspectives: timing, market demand, and competition.

- Identify the major competitors in your market, understand their plans, and build defense plans into your business from the beginning.

PART II

KNOW

CHAPTER 4

TIMING IS EVERYTHING

"In the publishing business, you're either first, you're fabulous, or you're f***ed!"

—ANONYMOUS

Everyone's heard the story about Isaac Newton sitting under an apple tree while developing the theory of gravity. Imagine the opportunities that existed in Newton's time, in the early days of modern science, to have a profound impact through relatively simple and foundational contributions. Today, you would need to deduce exceedingly complex theories about quantum physics and the existence of "god" particles to have even a fraction of the impact Newton had.

The same holds true today, at the end of the Internet's golden age. There are countless stories in recent memory of those who set up websites and made a million dollars. Google AdWords used to provide easy advertising opportunities in which lead generation and affiliate marketers could generate profound traffic—for pennies on the dollar of the income that traffic could generate. Even getting free traffic through Google's and Yahoo's organic search results was fairly easy, as the search algorithms were less sophisticated and the amount of competition was far less than now.

There was a popular idea floating around during the golden age that the Internet was the great equalizer. It brought democratization to the marketplace. It was the beginning of a new economy in which previous power structures were neutralized and anyone could start a business that reached everywhere, and had the same opportunity for success as anyone else. Ah, the good ol' days!

Today, the cost of AdWords equals or exceeds the value of the traffic it generates for many entrepreneurs (an issue of volume/size). Organic search results are heavily biased toward the largest and most established websites, with the proverbial wind of years of backlink history at their backs. Public companies have also started actively promoting their websites on television and through other major media, effectively doing end-runs around other online discovery-oriented channels. Not only has power begun to consolidate around major brands, there's also the issue of too much ambient noise. To illustrate this point, take a look at **Figure 4.1.** Netcraft.com has been keeping track of new websites since its inception and reports that, as of March 2012, there are 13 million active websites worldwide—a seven-fold increase since 2005.[1] No wonder it's begun to feel so crowded!

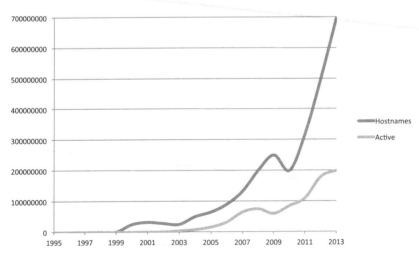

Figure 4.1 Active host names.

---

1 http://news.netcraft.com/archives/2012/03/05/march-2012-web-server-survey.html

In 2007, the iPhone, a new delivery platform, hit the market and instantly provided an unexploited opportunity to create content for these new devices. Those who moved quickly were able to garner the download counts that now drive placement in the App Store. Today, just five short years later, there are over 700,000 iPhone apps, and 60 percent of those actually lose money (compared to the cost of development).[2]

If we look at these examples, the immediate conclusion might be that it's too late to make any money online. It's not, though it *is* a lot more difficult if you weren't there in the beginning when the field was wide open.

Time and again, startups have made a lot of money very quickly by being at the right place, at the right time. This was true in the golden age of science, in the American industrial revolution, and in the Internet and mobile revolutions. Today the opportunities are smaller and require greater time and capital to be competitive. The rare exception is if your idea takes off in the social web. But for most it's a hard slog to see returns.

Against this backdrop, imagine what would be possible if you were in the right place at the right time. The good news is that innovation and opportunity are still happening around us all the time. The key is to find the emerging opportunities and align your startup with those opportunities. Let's take a look at a framework that can prove helpful.

Innovation adoption curve

In 1962, sociologist Everett Rogers developed the Innovation Adoption Curve, a bell curve distribution model that describes the absorption of innovation into culture. Geoffrey Moore further added an adoption chasm that exists between innovators and early adopters (**Figure 4.2**).

Rogers's and Moore's work has mostly been applied to the adoption of a specific technology or product, but it could also be applied to macro technologies and trends. For example, the Internet was originally developed by the U.S. Defense Advanced Research Projects Agency (DARPA) in the 1950s (innovators). It was improved through the use of TCP/IP protocols in 1982. But the first commercial applications didn't really begin until the introduction of Netscape in the early 1990s (early adopters), and it snowballed from there a few years later, as the early majorities arrived.

---

2 http://venturebeat.com/2012/05/04/ios-developers-lose-money/

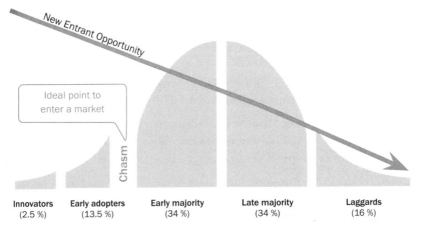

Figure 4.2 Everett Rogers's Innovation Adoption Curve.

This conceptual framework can be useful for analyzing timing of trends, in order to see the windows of entrepreneurial opportunity. We assume at a macro level that innovators are the academics and scientists creating pure innovation without application, the early adopters are the first to see opportunity for commercial application and either evangelize or commercialize it, and the consumers are the early/late majorities and laggards.

Take a look around your everyday life through the lens of this framework: Innovators are less than 2.5 percent of scientists and academics innovating without application. Early adopters follow with first attempts to apply the concepts with novelty products and in government defense work. The early majority are the first consumers to buy in, perhaps for social status purposes, similar to owning an iPhone in 2008. The late majority are busy pragmatists who cannot invest time until something has proven its value. And laggards are the grandparents who just signed up for Facebook to see the most recent pictures of the grandchildren.

There's something to be said for looking around you and observing the current level of adoption of an innovation before you attempt to commercialize it. The best commercial opportunities begin just as the late majority arrives, but you must have already built your product and gained some momentum before that time, which means you must be begin building your business before the early majority. And thus the chasm!

The chasm might also be ideal as you can minimize adoption risk by letting it play out just a little bit in that early adopter phase before investing yourself. Certainly, though, you would not want to enter the market after the late majority phase, as competitors are already entrenched and your window for capitalizing on the innovation before it is commoditized is minimal.

Perhaps the best recent example of this is the mobile market. In 2007 Apple introduced the iPhone and revolutionized the smartphone industry. But the raw innovation had been out there since the late 1990s. There were even HTTP and WAP-enabled phones prior to the iPhone, but none had gained much traction. These were the early adopters. The iPhone was the product that was needed to give enough bounce to overcome the chasm and lead the industry into early majority. Apple enjoyed dominance over the early majority phase until Google hit the market with Android, a free competitive platform, and this led to a proliferation of competitive devices and marked the beginning of the late majority phase. Android was able to compete because it's free and Google has massive pull as a company. The introduction of the Android platform marked the entry into the late majority and the beginning of commoditization of the industry.

The takeaway is that one can enter the market late, as Google did, but (a) you better have significant money to spend to build momentum and catch up, and (b) you should be a large business that can be a cost leader and make money on volume, since commoditization is soon to set in. Because of the late-market timing, your role will be to lead the commoditization on the way down the backside of the curve, not up. This is a role suitable only for a major organization, not a small startup that will need the early majority evangelists to gain momentum.

Commoditization of technology

"As information technology's power and ubiquity have grown, its strategic importance has diminished. The way you approach IT investment and management will need to change dramatically ... It is difficult to imagine a more perfect commodity than a byte of data—endlessly and perfectly reproducible at virtually no cost ... IT management should, frankly, become boring."

—Nicholas Carr

In an infamous article published in 2003 by the *Harvard Business Review*, Nicholas Carr asserted that information technology serves a similar purpose in industry as any other major technology has, such as railroads, the assembly line, or combustible engines. At first these innovations are proprietary and offer a substantial advantage in the market for those who possess this technology. But over time the technology becomes more common and standardized, providers more plentiful, competition rises, and consequently, the value of that technology becomes insignificant from a competitive perspective.

Commoditization of technology is all around us. For example, bandwidth and hosting costs are trivial now, compared to 10 years ago. So is the cost of a new laptop, unless you buy a Mac (an excellent example of positioning strategy at work). Apple has managed to escape the commodity vacuum arguably by making their products not about the technology. When you look at the now famous marketing of the iPod for example, it wasn't about gigabytes or megahertz. It was simply about "a thousand songs in your pocket." In this case, technology is the means, not the end goal.

If we look at Internet consulting firms today, it's not really about building a website any more. Outsourcing has certainly commoditized those skills, and open source software like WordPress and its free design themes have eased the design concerns for most low-budget websites. Even writing better code is less important now with cheap RAM, CPUs, and mature concepts of server clustering. Consulting firms that are still going strong in 2012 are those focusing on the application of technology for the purposes of marketing, not the production of it. SEO and social marketing firms are red hot in 2012. Even at the higher end of the market, IBM has shifted away from technology and toward strategy consulting. As IBM's strategic executive Irving Wladawsky-Berger noted in 2003, "We've entered the post-technology era."

An article written by Timothy M. Chester in the *Educause Quarterly* went as far as saying that educators need to be mindful of training "future technology advocates and CIO leaders, not the leaders of technology mechanics,"[3] further recognition that the tide has shifted toward strategic

---

3 Timothy M. Chester (2006), "A Roadmap for IT Leadership and the Next Ten Years," http://www.educause.edu/ero/article/roadmap-it-leadership-and-next-ten-years

use, not implementation. Chester suggests that projects and budgeting should no longer be considered IT projects, but rather as human resource projects, marketing projects, training products, and so forth, all of which utilize IT (a commodity resource) for their implementation, similar to how a house or office building project would implement electricity and plumbing.

In another interesting data point, Mark Suster of GRP Partners spoke about the explosion of technology entrepreneurship in the past 10 years.[4] He illustrates with a slideshow how substantially the cost of technology decreased for starting a business by 2011.[5] The proliferation of cloud computing, APIs (Application Programming Interfaces) for mashups, open source frameworks, and low-cost SaaS applications have dramatically reduced operating costs and increased opportunity to create compelling products by way of combining these technologies (**Figure 4.3**).

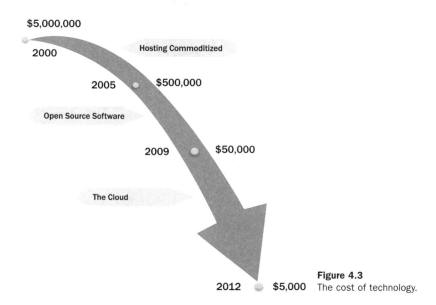

Figure 4.3
The cost of technology.

4 http://www.docstoc.com/docs/100225840/Future-of-VC-Internet
5 http://www.bothsidesofthetable.com/2011/10/20/5259/

Though the process of commoditization may have accelerated in recent years, the phenomenon is nothing new. As far back as 1823, others such as David Ricardo and Karl Marx pontificated the Law of Diminishing Returns, asserting that the profits for a given unit will eventually be reduced to the incremental cost of production for an additional unit. So if it costs $1 to produce an additional cup of coffee once the original template is perfected, then that is the eventual price target for that cup of coffee. Likewise, if the cost of reproduction for a unit of software is $0 (it costs nothing to digitally duplicate software), the eventual price target should be close or equal to $0 (**Figure 4.4**).

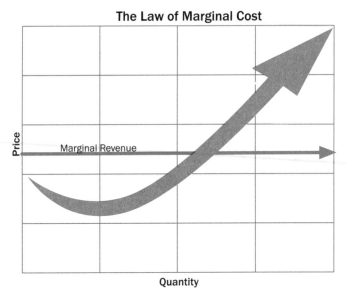

The Law of Marginal Cost

Price

Marginal Revenue

Quantity

Figure 4.4
Marginal cost.

Your products and even your business are inevitably headed toward commoditization unless you reinvest in them so that users get additional value when they buy from you. If you haven't reinvested by the time your products are commoditized, then you yourself have become a commodity. The only way to overcome this is to focus on the value you provide around that commodity. And yes, it is possible to do after the fact.

If you're a technologist or a technical entrepreneur, what do you do with this information? The lesson is not to avoid technology, but rather to build value *around* it, either with auxiliary services or by focusing your technology development efforts on how to augment existing commoditized technology, always innovating and staying a couple steps ahead of commoditization.

The value of network effects

Metcalfe's Law asserts that the power of a network is proportional to the square of the number of users connected to that network. It was originally calculated in the 1980s by George Gilder regarding telecommunications networks and later attributed to Robert Metcalfe.[6] It was referenced extensively for social networking sites during the Web 2.0 movement of the early 2000s.

It is considered to be a heuristic or metaphor, not a technically accurate model, but it does illustrate the significance of community adoption in the value of user adoption and what is otherwise called "networking effects."

When developing a business model with a dependence on social interaction, it's important to consider this dynamic carefully. If you are an early provider of a product or service, networking effects can have a profoundly positive effect on your business. Conversely, if you are a late entrant, this will be an exponentially negative effect and will cause significant difficulty in trying to penetrate your target market, particularly once the network has reached critical mass, which is when a sufficient amount of adopters of an innovation in a social system exist such that the rate of adoption becomes self-sustaining and creates further growth.

There were a couple lessons learned here. First, if you're a bootstrap company and are not first to market, avoid a business model that depends on networking effects; it is truly a tough paradox to overcome without resources. Second, if you're in such a market or have reasonable resources to overcome this initial challenge, look at how you can divide and conquer by appealing to specific segments one at a time.

---

6 http://en.wikipedia.org/wiki/Metcalfe%27s_law

Like every dynamic, network effects can be a powerful force if channeled properly. Look for opportunities to leverage networking effects if you have a relatively new or viral idea that people might want to identify with socially. The litmus test when applying networking effects to your business model is to ask yourself if there is something inherently viral about your product. You can validate your chances early by doing simple tests such as posting content and doing a few social experiments via Twitter and StumbleUpon.

Takeaways

- Timing is perhaps the single greatest factor in whether your business will be successful. Use Rogers's Innovation Adoption Curve to identify the current stage of the life cycle a business to determine if timing is favorable.

- The cost of starting a business is lower than ever. While this presents a fantastic opportunity for entrepreneurs, it also means that competition is higher than ever.

- Understand Metcalfe's Law and avoid network effects businesses unless you're very early in the market cycle.

- Understand the effects of commoditization on your ability to enter a market profitably. Look carefully for signs of commoditization when validating opportunity.

CHAPTER 5

COMPETITION AND POSITIONING

"It is said that if you know your enemies and know yourself, you will not be imperiled in a hundred battles; if you do not know your enemies but do know yourself, you will win one and lose one; if you do not know your enemies nor yourself, you will be imperiled in every single battle ... A general is skillful in attack whose opponent does not know what to defend; and he is skillful in defense whose opponent does not know what to attack."

—SUN TZU

An inexperienced entrepreneur focuses exclusively on building a great product, finding product-market fit, and improving user experience. While these are excellent goals, they assume that entrepreneurship occurs in a vacuum, without the effects of any competition. That can be a correct strategy if yours is the first product in a market and you don't need to differentiate yourself or defend yourself from others seeking to differentiate, but as the Internet matures and entrepreneurial competition for every online market segment grows, the odds of happening on such a context are increasingly low.

Every entrepreneur needs to be aware of the fundamentals of competitive analysis and positioning strategy in order to identify and correctly respond to the competition he or she faces. Imagine the value of realizing that a market you were about to enter was not viable before you spent all of your resources fighting that battle you could not win. If you study the competition and recognize the patterns of consolidation of a marketplace, you create opportunities to preserve resources and find other opportunities, thus increasing your ultimate odds of success.

In this chapter, we'll cover competitive analysis, positioning strategy, value chain, commoditization, and network effects as core concepts for competitive positioning. We'll introduce a few well-regarded academic models that can be useful for understanding and analyzing ecosystems, actionable frameworks, and case studies to demonstrate how these models apply.

Competitive strategy

When entering a market, it helps to understand the relative opportunities, costs, and risks before proceeding. By understanding the dynamics of a market, you can determine whether it makes sense to enter the market and, if so, how to proceed.

Porter's Five Forces

In 1980, renowned economist and Harvard Business School professor Michael Porter introduced a competitive analysis model called the Five Forces, in a book titled *Competitive Strategy: Techniques for Analyzing Industries and Competitors.* This model applies microeconomic principles to create a framework by which to analyze the competitive landscape of a market and better equip strategists to plot their course (**Figure 5.1**). It describes the need to analyze the changing dynamics and continuous flux between and within the forces:

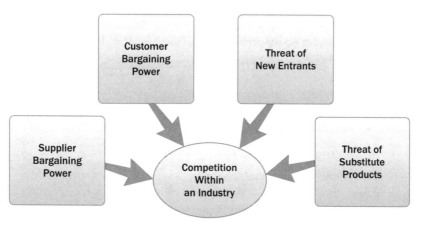

Figure 5.1 Porter's Five Forces.

1. Threat of new entrants (or competitors)

   A market that hosts a successful company that is generating high profits will naturally attract other competition to the market. Other entrepreneurs will observe and want to copy the success of that company. In turn, the market will grow full of competitors who competitively squeeze margins, and eventually will decrease profitability for all in the industry, unless there is some key detractor preventing it. Provided your goal is to create a company with long-term profit potential, you would want to create the barriers to entry, which can mitigate the crowding of your market, where few new companies can enter and nonperforming companies can exit early. These barriers to entry then become your competitive advantage.

2. Threat of substitute products (or services)

   The question is not whether a competitor with an equal product might displace you. Rather, what is the risk of the entire market segment that you serve being displaced? For example, if you are an aluminum can manufacturer, what is the possibility of glass bottles growing in popularity and thus reducing opportunity in your market segment?

3. Bargaining power of customers

   How much power does your customer have over price and terms? This is both a question of organization and of supply versus demand. If your customers are organized and represent a larger portion of market, they have "purchase power." An example might be a real estate association that represents all local Realtors and is negotiating for a bulk price for a given technology package. Another reason for customer power would be a greater quantity of suppliers than buyers. In such a case, suppliers will compete fiercely for each competitor, including competition on price. This implicitly gives the customer bargaining power.

4. Bargaining power of suppliers

   The inverse of customer bargaining power is supplier bargaining power, though the dynamics are somewhat different. If customers depend heavily on the supplier or switching costs are too high, preventing customers from switching to another supplier, this favors the supplier, as does a lack of alternatives.

5. Competitive rivalry of market

   Through the above forces a market dynamic is created and the intensity of competition among rivals in that market is the ultimate basis on which most businesses will determine whether to enter a market. Factors to consider at this level are market fragmentation or consolidation, opportunity for sustainable competitive advantage through ongoing innovation or technology improvements, customer acquisition costs, and competitors' financial resources.

The Five Forces model is not a precise formula that can give you a prescribed course of action by inputting specific variables, but it is an excellent construct for analyzing a market. The deeper you analyze a market, the more value the construct becomes, specifically as you begin to look at the issue of interplay between market forces. Of course, nothing is static in markets.

Generic competitive strategy

That same year, Porter introduced the Generic Competitive Strategy model, which identifies a generally applicable competitive strategy that individual companies could build upon (**Figure 5.2**). The three components of this model are: segmentation, differentiation, and cost leadership. After initially beginning with a 3 x 3 x 3 cube defining 27 possible strategies, Porter eventually invalidated all but three and concluded there are only three valid strategies applicable across market segments:

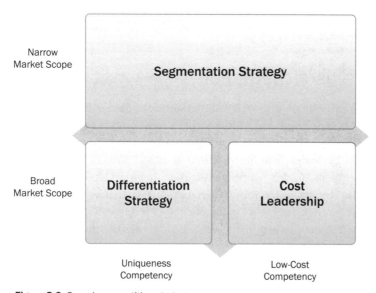

Figure 5.2 Generic competitive strategy.

1. Cost leadership

    The dominant brand in a market naturally focuses on scale to maximize profit. As a result of building scale, the brand can compete on price that no one else can match. This is the ultimate defensible position and is maximally profitable due to volume.

2. Differentiation

   Find something unique about your product so that it is not in the same category as the cost leader. This is the preferred method for a secondary competitor that has resources to reach a large market but needs to protect a product (or service) from the commoditization trap.

3. Segmentation

   Focus on a specific niche audience. With resources, one can be much more effective by focusing on a smaller market segment. This is the preferred strategy for startups, when primary and secondary competitors already exist.

Warfare as a metaphor

Focusing specifically on the rivalry of markets described in the Five Forces model, Jack Trout and Al Ries wrote a now famous book titled *Marketing Warfare*. The book is now a staple of business strategy and derives strategy models from nearly three thousand years of military strategy to provide models for predicting outcomes and blueprints for corporate strategies. The foundational premise is that business competition is war. Concerning yourself only with innovation or exceeding customer expectations is insufficient, as it ignores the threats of your competitors.

The battle being fought by marketers is for mindshare. It has been said that a brand can only be successfully attributed to a single application. For example, Coke for cola or Kleenex for tissue or Google for Internet search. In an effort to contend with information overload, consumers tend to cluster brands around specific functions or values in their life and prioritize those brands accordingly.

It's much easier to defend a position of dominance than to compete for dominance. In *The Art of War*, Sun Tzu said the first competitors to the field commanded the advantage, as they can set up camp, identify and control their geographic weaknesses, and implement trenches from which to assault the enemy. Likewise, entrenched business competitors have many similar advantages. Thus, it is assumed that to attack an entrenched competitor, you must overwhelm them, either with force or resources. Similarly, consider the financial resources required for a new brand to enter an established market and grab the attention of consumers who already have attached the market segment to dominant brands.

Distribution of market share typically follows a 4:2:1 ratio. In other words, the primary brand will command twice as much market share as the secondary competitor and four times as much market share as the tertiary competitor. So if the top brand maintains 50 percent market share, the second most powerful brand would control only 25 percent market share, and number three might have 12.5 percent market share. That leaves only 12.5 percent of the market for all remaining competitors to fight over. Thus it is critical to be as high up that food chain as possible, even if it means taking a divide-and-conquer approach to further segmentation of an existing segment. If you can dominate a small segment, you're likely still better off compared to being number three for a larger segment.

Trout and Ries describe a strategic square, which outlines four possible postures a brand might assume, depending on the position they currently occupy in the market segment. The four possible strategies are as follows:

1. **Defensive**

   The dominant market segment brand should focus on defending its market dominance. At some point it cannot continue offensive aggression for fear of government regulation and anti-competitive issues. Thus the focus is on blocking aggression from contending competitors.

2. **Offensive**

   The goal of the next nearest competitor should be direct competition. The value of fighting for market share as the number three competitor is not substantial enough to be worth the cost of a battle, whereas even a small market share win from the second position brand may pay off.

3. **Flanking**

   The number three competitor does not have the resources or power for a sustained attack on the primary or secondary brands. It is better off initiating tangential battles to the sides of the primary battleground—areas that are not yet controlled by an existing brand. If the number three competitor can establish a foothold in a tangential segment, it is in a better position to fight a larger offensive battle later.

4. Guerilla

Guerilla marketing is for the smallest and newest entrants who cannot afford a battle of any sort. Paul Graham of Y Combinator once advised some of his young startups to do things that don't scale.[1] The implication is to seek market subsegments that are either too small or too inefficient for the larger competitors to notice or take interest in. Since these small competitors have no resources for a battle, the strategy is to avoid confrontation.

These military insights can be of significant value in identifying the competitive ecosystem of a given market and determining effective strategy within an ecosystem, based on your ability to compete and capture mindshare. In the next section, we'll look at tactical models that can be applied specifically to positioning your brand effectively.

Positioning strategy

Positioning is the art of creating an identity for your brand, differentiating it from stronger competitors and aligning with preferential brands from tangential markets. If you are able to identify your key strengths and focus your marketing message around those, you can be the best in a category that you define, rather than third or fourth in a category someone else controls. Conversely, if you can associate with tangential brands, you can leverage their brand goodwill to get an edge in winning over those customers.

The importance of positioning strategy goes back to the 4:2:1 ratio mentioned in the previous section, in which market share is dominated by the top three brands of a market, in a 4:2:1 ratio, leaving the remaining brands to compete over the remaining small market opportunity. You are generally better off to be the first in a small category than fourth in a large category.

The goal of positioning is to be the first brand that a consumer thinks of when a need comes to mind. This is true for both well-defined niche service businesses and consumer products. This is why it is preferable to be a primary brand in a smaller niche, rather than third or fourth in a larger segment; at least you will be the primary brand in someone's mind, some

---

1 http://mixergy.com/airbnb-chesky-gebbia/

of the time. This is why even large companies like Procter & Gamble market smaller segment-specific brands such as Crest for toothpaste, Herbal Essences for hairspray, and Covergirl for cosmetics. Some online companies have advocated the same for their online products, such as 37signals' popular Basecamp project management and Highrise CRM products.

It is essential that every brand have a clear concept of what the brand is and what it stands for. If you do not define your own brand position, you risk someone else doing it for you. In the book *22 Immutable Laws of Marketing,* Al Ries and Jack Trout describe how one brand can implicitly reposition another in a negative way. When Scope entered the mouthwash market, it indirectly challenged the leader Listerine by referring to itself as the "good-tasting mouthwash," an obvious jab at Listerine's harsh flavor. This worked for a short while until Listerine defended itself with an equally indirect slogan that declared "you can feel it working," implying that Scope was ineffective.

At a high level there are three types of positioning concepts:

1. Functional (logical)

   Your product solves a problem that others do not, or solves it better. This can be a precious position to hold as it provides for easy comparison and commoditization later in market maturity. Early in a market life cycle, however, it can be the most effective way to introduce a new market segment and take ownership of it. IBM was successful as the original computer brand and AOL as the original Internet service provider. You don't need to actually be the first on the market; you need to be first in the mind of your consumer.

2. Symbolic (ego)

   Take ownership of a personality or status symbol in a market. The easiest way to differentiate is often by becoming the premium alternative to the functional alternative. BMW does this with cars and Chanel with handbags.

3. Experience (lifestyle)

   Lifestyle marketing is less about appealing to ego and more about improving the user experience. Apple introduced better user experience to computers; Starbucks augmented the value chain around a commodity product of coffee, so the store became a destination and a part of consumers' morning routine.

In 2001, Michael Porter introduced the Six Principles of Strategic Positioning. Now that we've covered the basics of competition and positioning, this framework provides a good framework for how to apply positioning to your brand in the real world:[2]

1. Goals

   You cannot execute a clear or effective strategy unless the underlying objective of that strategy is clear. The goals must be aligned with the long-term, sustainable profitability of the organization, not short-term, tactical goals such as traffic acquisition.

2. Value proposition

   The strategy must define a set of benefits or value that will be delivered to a specific target market. Don't try to be all things to all people. The goal is to identify how you will be more relevant to a specific market segment than everyone else, and how you will deliver greater value to that specific segment.

3. Distinctive value chain

   Value chain describes the additional value an organization can bring to a product or service through its additional offerings or fulfillment. For example, Starbucks did a masterful job of wrapping coffee, a commodity, in an exceptional user experience through gourmet drinks and an inviting atmosphere where customers could relax and socialize. Zappos augmented its value chain through exceptional customer support and return policies, taking the risk out of buying shoes online. This differs from a unique value proposition in that the company is improving the overall value of a product with its value chain, not by segmenting the audience.

4. Trade-offs

   To excel at one thing, a company must not be distracted or bogged down by other things. To be the best at a specific value proposition for a specific segmented audience, you may need to give up features that are common with competitors but not critical to your segmented audience. Not only does this serve the pragmatic goal of helping the company to focus, it also focuses the brand position in the mind of the consumer.

---

2 Michael Porter (2001), "Strategy and the Internet," *Harvard Business Review*, vol. 79, no. 3, March 2001

5. Cohesiveness

Speak with one voice. Your design needs to reinforce your marketing copy, which needs to reinforce the functional concept of your product, your customer experience, and so on. In other words, let your positioning strategy drive tactical implementation of every aspect of your product and business. Only then will you have a consistent and authentic brand that a customer will relate to after interacting with your product or service.

6. Continuity

Stick with it. For a brand position to be effective, it must be stable and have time to incubate in the minds of your customers. A brand that continually reinvents itself stands for nothing. Reinvention is fine in the early stages of finding product/market fit, but once a brand is mature enough to be concerned with owning a position in the market, all of your positioning efforts are futile if you don't stick with it and act authentic.

Mind your value chain

Amazon.com is famous for its relentless reinvestment into its operations in the early 2000s, amid a backdrop of dot-com ruin and with its shareholders demanding profit distributions. At some level it's obvious what the company was up to—it wanted to seize the opportunity to become the biggest, baddest e-retailer on the planet. Amazon was early in the game and wanted to seize the opportunity before it passed. And with the down recession market suppressing competitive reinvestment, it further increased that opportunity to grow to a dominant position.

In 1979, Michael Porter introduced the idea of the Value Chain, suggesting there are multiple layers of your business that go into creating the customer experience, and each layer that the product passes through adds value (**Figure 5.3**). For example, those sourcing connections and preferred pricing structures are worth something, but so are the IT system that enables quick fulfillment and the premium customer support that you provide compared to your competition. Each of these layers augments the value of the final product to your customer.

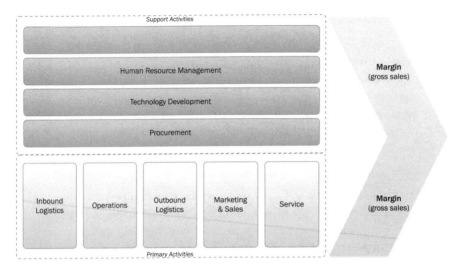

Figure 5.3 Value chain.

What Amazon.com did was take the opportunity to master its value chain before anyone else did. It perfected its supply chain, shopping experience, and upsell/recommendations engine, and defined an industry-leading returns and customer support process. The end result was a company with a world-class operation that stood for trust and reliability and helped prospects to overcome the fear of entering their credit card numbers online years before anyone else.

This earned the company significant brand value, which led to higher conversion rates and thus fed back into the value proposition (trust value feedback loop). It was then able to leverage its dominant position and purchase volume, to drive prices lower than just about anyone except perhaps Walmart.

And now that Amazon is in this position, how do you compete? Well, you don't. The barriers to entry it has created through years of reinvestment and growth are enormous. The brand value and sourcing advantages make it nearly impossible for anyone to compete with it head-on as a volume supplier. Those are massively defensible positions, and so the company's future is theirs to lose. The best opportunity for another online retailer would be to go around Amazon, not to compete head-on.

And what about companies that didn't make these investments at that critical time? Their products are simply worth less to the end consumer. Chances are, if they compete directly with Amazon, they're earning less now, which means something else has to give: infrastructure, return policies, support, or something else. As a result, their value will diminish over time until they are completely marginalized.

Starbucks is another interesting example. The company took a product that had only marginally capitalizable value and created value *around* it in a way that was completely innovative, particularly in the U.S. where cafés rarely existed before. It took a commodity and created a value chain around it. And by building around a commodity rather than the latest thing, it was virtually uncontested in its market and under the radar until it established critical mass and no one could take that market away.

Instead of being just a coffee bar, Starbucks created gourmet drinks— which just happened to be based on coffee. It created inviting spaces with nice comfortable chairs and ambient music that are enjoyable to hang out in. It created a place for people to congregate and socialize. It created a lifestyle brand that people could identify with, thus engaging an entirely new generation of coffee drinkers. By creating all of this, the coffee was of secondary significance. What people are paying for when they purchase a $4 cup of coffee is the value that has been created *around* the cup of coffee, not just the coffee itself. And yet by anchoring the entire concept around a known commodity with established demand, the company was able to establish a brand that resonated. Again, this was much easier than trying to create an entirely new market and convince users of its value while simultaneously competing with numerous well-funded companies for mindshare.

Zappos arguably accomplished the same thing in the retail space. It sells shoes, and not even unique ones; it's merely a shoe reseller. Sure, it was able to achieve enough scale to negotiate preferential sourcing and pricing, but that's barely enough to stay above the fray of commoditization. What really separated Zappos and allowed it to soar was its amazing customer service. The company created value around the shoes by reducing the risk of online purchases and enhancing the overall shopping experience for customers. It's no longer just selling a commodity, and the customer gets more value in that experience than a mere pair of shoes. It's now able to compete without reducing prices.

What both Zappos and Starbucks did is simple. They took a stagnant commodity with known demand and built a value chain around it. They looked at how to increase value around that commodity and launched a new premium opportunity within their market segment. Apple has done the same with commoditizing computer equipment. All of these companies identified innovative ways to bring new value to existing market segments, rather than just being another me-too brand doing more of the same. Perhaps this sort of innovation is where the real opportunities of our generation lie—not in creating another iPhone productivity app (there are over 700,000 apps in the iTunes store as of this writing).

Takeaways

- Use core business strategies such as Porter's Five Forces and Generic Competitive Strategy to understand the competition and create effective market positioning.

- The best position to be in is the cost leader, followed by a differentiated position. If no differentiation exists, segment the market for a better share of a smaller market.

- Market share allocation is disproportionately awarded to the leaders of a given market. It's better to be the first brand in a smaller category than to not be in the top three of a larger one.

- When a brand builds its value chain, it's more desirable to customers and less sensitive to price competition.

CHAPTER 6

BUSINESS MODELS

"There's not a single business model, and there's not a single type of electronic content. There are really a lot of opportunities and a lot of options and we just have to discover all of them."

—TIM O'REILLY

A business model describes how an organization creates, captures, and delivers value to its customers. Every business performs some activity with the intention of generating value for its customers. At a conceptual level, what does that look like and what existing businesses can you point to as examples to determine that your model is sound?

Identifying your business model is helpful for two important reasons. First, by studying businesses with a similar business model, you can increase your own odds of success—an activity referred to as modeling. Second, it provides a blueprint by which you can begin taking action to define your business model. If you already have a model, you still can make improvements or reinvent it by comparing it to well-established models—an activity referred to as benchmarking.

Seven business model archetypes

After spending considerable time mapping the various business models online, we began to realize that many of the models were similar. We observed there are fundamentally three archetypes that drive all business models: Trade, Product, and Service. This was a breakthrough observation for us, because it paved the way for the model we then created.

Just as a color wheel starts with three primary colors and derives a set of basic colors from the original three (red, green, blue), we've done the same with our model. Many of the interesting online businesses are hybrids of two of the three primaries; we call these the hybrid archetypes. They include the Marketplace, Brokerage, and Subscription models. And lastly there is the Ecosystem, which possesses traits of all three primary archetypes.

Figure 6.1 illustrates this framework, which can be a useful place to start thinking about how to structure your business. To make this framework more useful, we also overlaid two prototypes to demonstrate each archetype. These prototypes are more defined and actionable models of the more abstract archetype concept. This is not an exhaustive list of possible prototypes, just a set of examples that illustrate the concept and provide actionable material that you can use. Following the detailed description of each archetype, we provide a list of the prototypes and a set of examples for each that appear to be succeeding online.

Trade

Trade is the primary archetype that describes the business of connecting buyers and sellers, rather than offering something to be bought or sold. The trader is the consummate "connector" who knows everyone and helps to make introductions. Profits are generated by commission or arbitrage, not by selling units or hours.

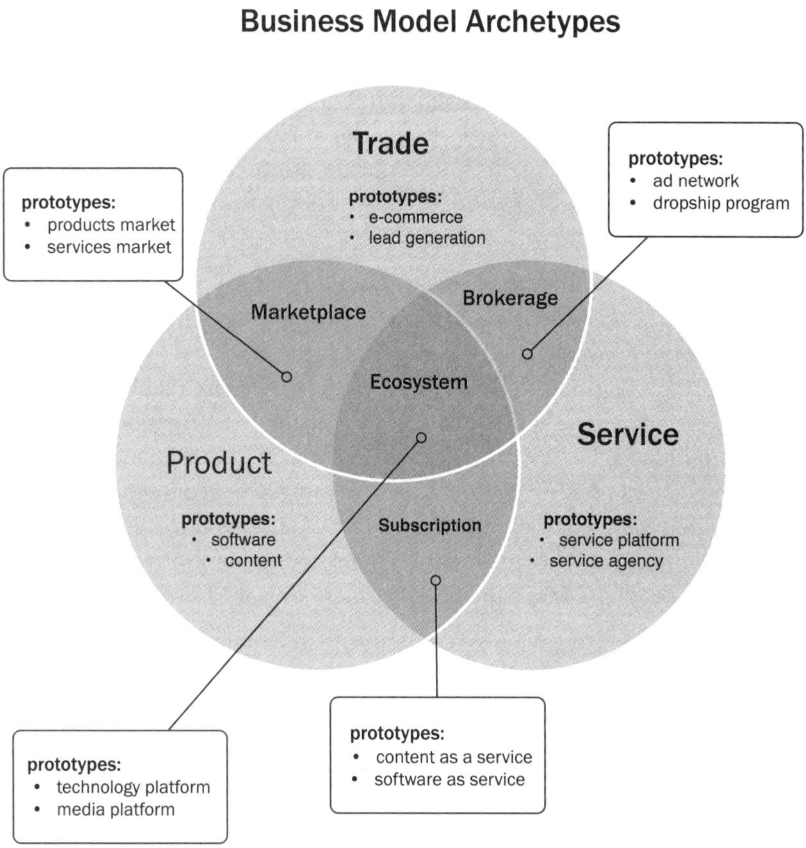

Business Model Archetypes

prototypes:
- products market
- services market

Trade

prototypes:
- e-commerce
- lead generation

prototypes:
- ad network
- dropship program

Marketplace

Brokerage

Ecosystem

Product

prototypes:
- software
- content

Subscription

Service

prototypes:
- service platform
- service agency

prototypes:
- technology platform
- media platform

prototypes:
- content as a service
- software as service

Figure 6.1 Online business models.

The ideal trader personality is typically someone who comes from a business background, who's comfortable reaching out to people, and who knows how to run complex spreadsheets. The trader's core activities involve sales and sourcing, and the focus of the business is minding the spread between the two, in order to maintain optimal profitability.

The two prototypes for the Trade Archetype are ecommerce and lead generation. While ecommerce focuses on physical products and lead generation on media arbitrage, they both demonstrate the same core arbitrage activity: buying inventory, packaging it, and reselling it for a higher price.

ECOMMERCE

Ecommerce is a straightforward retail model, applied online. A business sources products, advertises to generate traffic, and sells the products online. The activities are equally straightforward to understand, and success depends on the ability to source quality products and quality traffic at a low cost and use the website to maximize the transactions that come from pairing products with traffic.

The two main types of ecommerce websites are large volume and boutique. The large volume merchant can sell products at a low cost but depends on selling very large quantities of these products to make money, since each transaction is of relatively low value. The emergence of powerful, large-volume merchants such as Amazon.com and Target.com have made it increasingly difficult for smaller merchants to make money simply by buying and selling commodity or brand-name products, since they lack the volume to compete with the prices of large-volume businesses. Instead, boutique merchants focus on being a dominant provider of just one or two products, since they can compete on volume this way.

A key competitive advantage for the online merchant is sourcing cost. The merchant also needs to be highly proficient in online marketing channels (keyword research, pay-per-click campaigns, landing page optimization, and so on) in order to keep margins under control. This reflects the fundamental nature of cost arbitrage at the core of the Trade Archetype.

Table 6.1 Key attributes and strategies for ecommerce

ATTRIBUTES	STRATEGIES
Key partners	Product sourcing and advertising
Value proposition	Low price, convenience, and curation
Key activities	Sourcing and advertising
Monetization	Product arbitrage

LEAD GENERATION

A lead-generation business does not create or stock its own product. It is focused on generating and qualifying leads that can be sold to its business partners. With this model the lead generator is neither consultant nor service provider to its business partners; rather, it is selling the leads on a per-unit basis, for a fee commonly called a "bounty."

The sophistication and approach of lead-generation companies varies widely, but the goal is always the same: generate qualified leads and sell them to a handful of clients at a marked-up premium. In a way, lead generation can be thought of as arbitraging the online ad markets in much the same way as the stock market. The traffic is acquired through a common media channel, scored and qualified, and then repackaged into a more meaningful and higher-quality unit that is actionable by the sales force of the acquiring company.

In the early days of the Internet, there were few who understood online marketing. For those who did blaze the early trails, there was considerable money to be made. Today the landscape is more challenging, but the nimble lead generator can still stay a couple steps ahead and perform advertisement arbitrage on newer media channels. Over the longer term, it's important to create end-user value in order to obtain traffic and retain visitors. The emphasis in lead generation (and affiliate marketing, its close relative) has thus shifted toward content creation as a vehicle to attain organic search results and to provide a vehicle for social and email marketing. Professional bloggers, for example, frequently monetize their content using lead generation-related activities.

Table 6.2 Key attributes and strategies for lead generation

ATTRIBUTES	STRATEGIES
Key partners	Sales departments
Value proposition	Demand generation
Key activities	Media buying
Monetization	Media arbitrage

Product

The Product is the primary archetype that describes the creation of a tangible unit of value that can be bought and sold in a marketplace. The product creator is typically an engineer, intellectual, or artist who is compelled to create something. The product itself might efficiently solve a problem in the case of an engineer, or might intrigue or entertain in the case of an intellectual or artist.

Profits are generated through sale of a sufficient quantity to overcome initial sunk cost requirements to set up and produce the product. Since the product must be created before it can be demonstrated or sold, there can be a significant risk burden for the product entrepreneur. For this reason, it is common for product businesses to seek investors to fund product development and expansion costs.

The reason digital products attract so many funding opportunities is because of the ability to quickly and cost-effectively scale. Once the initial cost and risk burdens are overcome, a product business has the potential to grow quickly and provide a substantial return on the initial investment, within a relatively short period of time. While this is highly attractive to investors, it does come at a long-term cost. Because products are easily reproduced, they are also easily copied and thus vulnerable to commoditization, as a result of too much competition entering a market. As quickly as a business can ramp up, so too can it fall when equally funded competition enters the market.

For this reason, digital products are a high-stakes and high-reward opportunity. Timing of market entry is particularly important and so is having sufficient capital to compete. The business must fight aggressively to establish dominance quickly so as to sell large quantities of product at a maximally compressed profit margin.

SOFTWARE AS A PRODUCT

A software product is purchased for a one-time fee from an online marketplace. It is then downloaded and installed on an individual computer or server. Software as a product in its purest form is best demonstrated by how Microsoft sold software in the 1990s. The product was created, boxed, and distributed to physical stores; it was inherently tangible.

Today most software is sold in online marketplaces, so the product is not as tangible. We still define it as a product, however, because it has a user interface and turnkey functionality. Common manifestations of the software product are mobile apps in the consumer world, and functional plug-ins and design themes for software platforms such as Magento and Salesforce in the business world.

Table 6.3 Key attributes and strategies for software

ATTRIBUTES	STRATEGIES
Key partners	Marketplaces
Value proposition	Cost-effective productivity
Key activities	Software development
Monetization	Sale of product

CONTENT AS A PRODUCT

Content as a product is any form of intellectual property that can be bought or sold in a marketplace. Common offline product examples include books, music CDs, TV shows, and movies on DVD. Applying this concept to online, we are limited to digital media that can be bought and sold primarily through online marketplaces such as e-books, MP3s, or videos.

This is the ideal domain for the intellectual or artistic entrepreneur who wants to develop and sell his ideas, particularly in the digital era. Several recent innovations have led to the democratization of media content and now are in the favor of small, independent content producers. First, with the advent of digital technology, the cost of producing high-quality products is substantially lower than it was even just a decade ago. Second, marketplace distribution that was once limited to those few who were signed by major media companies is now accessible to anyone with a computer and some initiative.

The major challenge for those creating content products is breaking through the noise. Because product development and distribution costs have fallen so much, there is a glut of content products on the market. This also means that many original ideas have already been explored. The burden for the content product creator thus is to create compelling content that is fresh and will stand out from the crowd.

Several companies have built brands around content creation, such as Advantage Media, which helps entrepreneurs to write and publish e-books, and Maker Studios for development of YouTube content. Meanwhile, many believe the technology for the coming convergence of the Internet and television is already in place and a wave of innovation is imminent, which will create tremendous new opportunities in this area.[1]

---

1 http://www.bothsidesofthetable.com/2011/11/14/future-of-tv-the-quick-version/

Table 6.4 Key attributes and strategies for content

ATTRIBUTES	STRATEGIES
Key partners	Marketplaces and ecosystems
Value proposition	Engaging content
Key activities	Writing, filming, and recording
Monetization	Product sale and ad revenue

Service

Service, the third primary archetype, provides intangible solutions for clients. The service provider is typically a group of skilled professionals or technicians with expert knowledge in a specific domain. Clients delegate responsibilities to the service provider because they require the competence or efficiency of a specialist.

Services fill the gap where existing off-the-shelf products do not satisfy a need, or for which customizations to that product are needed. They might also provide ongoing support, either as a skilled technician or an automated system.

SERVICE AGENCY

The Service Agency prototype consists of a team of skilled professionals who work on behalf of a client to solve specific problems dictated by the client, on an hourly or project basis. This can be in the form of consulting and training, or as a production agency, performing specialty work on behalf of a client who does not retain those specialty skills in-house.

For engagements in which the vendor has performed similar work before, it's common to charge fixed rates for services rendered. Many consulting and production opportunities are unique, however, and requirement discovery is a big part of the engagement. In such cases, the agency typically bills on a time and materials basis (that is, hourly plus expenses).

For both of these agency models, it's important to develop a platform for services to avoid being marginalized. For consultants, this is accomplished through publishing and speaking engagements that raise awareness and pedigree. For the agency, this might be accomplished through strategic partnerships and independent service vendor (ISV) relationships.

Table 6.5 Key attributes and strategies for service agency

ATTRIBUTES	STRATEGIES
Key partners	Ecosystem platform owner
Value proposition	Customization and support of platform
Key activities	Customization and maintenance
Monetization	Time and materials

SERVICE PLATFORM (PAAS)

The Service Platform prototype is synonymous with the Platform as a Service model (PaaS). The Internet's cloud architecture consists of three layers: service, platform, and infrastructure. At the top of the stack are Software as a Service (SaaS) providers offering customer-facing applications such as CRMs, social networks, productivity tools, and so on. Just below that are Platform as a Service (PaaS) providers who offer outsourced resources to effectively power an SaaS business. In this way, PaaS is a decisively business-to-business focused business model, targeting primarily the developers of software solutions.

Examples of successful PaaS businesses include SendGrid for managed email services, DemandWare for ecommerce back-end services, and MaxMind for GEO IP and fraud detection. All three provide extensive API resources that custom applications can be written around, providing the opportunity to write automation around their outsourced services.

It may be tempting to think of PaaS as a hybrid product model, similar to SaaS. But keep in mind that what separates products from services is tangibility. SaaS may not sell in a marketplace like a true software product, but it does have a tangible user interface with turnkey user functionality, both of which are aspects of a product. Combine that with the ongoing maintenance and support and it is a clear hybrid of product and service. PaaS conversely lacks the tangible user interface and turnkey product attributes. It is typically consumed by applications via API. Thus it is a utility service.

Table 6.6 Key attributes and strategies for service platform

ATTRIBUTES	STRATEGIES
Key partners	IaaS providers
Value proposition	Outsourced management of service via API
Key activities	Maintain stability, scalability, and system health
Monetization	API pay per use

Marketplace

An online marketplace brings buyers of products together with sellers, providing a forum in which to conduct business. The Marketplace Archetype is considered a hybrid of the Trade and Product archetypes because it provides a fundamental service of putting buyers and sellers together, but it does so via a tangible "self-service" forum, which in itself is a product. The offline world's analog version of the online marketplace would be a farmer's market or a shopping mall.

The marketplace itself provides value by advertising and creating traffic for the benefit of buyers and sellers. As the marketplace grows larger, its value increases for everyone involved. This is a classic example of Metcalfe's Law regarding network effects, which suggests that a network is as valuable as the square of the number of participants. In other words, maximum value is not realized (conversion rates typically do not maximize and top clients do not opt in) until critical mass is achieved. While a marketplace can be a valuable and self-sustaining business once it achieves critical mass, it can be difficult to start for the same reasons.

PRODUCT MARKETPLACE

An effective product marketplace is typically utilized by small businesses as a means of selling their product(s). The best-known example of a product marketplace is eBay.com, which provides an auction platform for buyers and sellers to exchange goods all over the world. It is dominated by small resellers, and the company has augmented the marketplace for that core audience by offering Pro Stores and PayPal for payment management.

Product marketplaces are also commonly found as an extension of the Ecosystem Archetype. Apple's App Store, Magento's Connect, and

Salesforce's Force.com are all examples. Third-party solution providers and service agencies create extension products for the ecosystem platform and sell their products through their marketplace.

Table 6.7 Key attributes and strategies for product marketplace

ATTRIBUTES	STRATEGIES
Key partners	Merchants (sellers)
Value proposition	Destination shopping
Key activities	Recruit vendors and advertise
Monetization	Commission per sale

SERVICE MARKETPLACE

The service marketplace is similar to the product marketplace, except the connections being created are clients and service providers, rather than customers and merchants. The prospective client has the advantage of selecting from a large pool of candidates and easily filtering and comparing them by specific criteria. It is common for service marketplaces to provide tests and certifications that professionals can take to demonstrate their abilities. It is also common practice for previous clients to rate the service provider, which helps prospective clients locate the best professional to assist them.

The marketplace business profits when a connection is made by taking a commission from hours billed and frequently offers related services such as hours tracking and escrow services. This model is common in software development and design, with brands such as oDesk and Freelancer being popular marketplaces for offshore talent. Elance meanwhile is popular with domestic professionals. Care.com is another great resource, focusing on nannies and adult care professionals.

Table 6.8 Key attributes and strategies for service marketplace

ATTRIBUTES	STRATEGIES
Key partners	Service providers (sellers)
Value proposition	Locate skilled professionals
Key activities	Recruit professionals and advertise for clients
Monetization	Commission per sale

Brokerage

The Brokerage Archetype is a hybrid of the Trade and Service archetypes. It provides trade as a service, on behalf of its clients. An advertiser may create content, purchase media, and conduct other activities with the end goal of generating traffic and demand for her clients.

As compared to the Trade Archetype, the performance incentive rests with the Brokerage because the broker sells a unit of inventory (product or media) at a market rate to a competing customer and profits from sourcing it lower than market rate. With a Brokerage, the effort is performed on behalf of a longer-term *client*, either for an agreed retainer or on a time and materials basis. Any profits generated due to the sourcing efforts are retained by the client.

Compare this also to a service agency that may create advertising content, design, and strategy for a brand, as a service company. While this type of service agency may specialize in the field of online advertising, the focus is on production skills and content strategy. In contrast, a true advertising company specializes in the brokering of media. It may also invest in brokering networks (ad networks), whereas the agency would focus more on effective communication and content.

ADVERTISING NETWORK

In its most primitive form, the advertising company connects those who want to advertise with those who want to monetize their online property through advertising. To better help advertisers navigate the complexities of online advertising, an advertising network becomes a common mediator of supply and demand. The company matches the most effective channels for a brand or product, and sources the advertising opportunity at the best price.

These activities were typically handled by a media-buying specialist in the offline world, but automation facilitates much of the online media brokering activity, including the selection of appropriate online properties and price negotiation. Traditional media buyers do still assemble custom media packages for large clients but, for most, the automation of the network proves the most efficient and cost-effective option.

Table 6.9 Key attributes and strategies for advertising network

ATTRIBUTES	STRATEGIES
Key partners	Media sites
Value proposition	Efficient media procurement
Key activities	Recruiting media sites
Monetization	Base fee plus commission

DROPSHIP PROGRAM

Today it's easier than ever to launch a retail business. Subscription ecommerce platforms make it possible for a business to launch an online store in 30 minutes or less and for as little as $20 per month. Companies like Volusion, BigCommerce, and Shopify take care of all of the mechanical details of getting a website up and running, even providing design themes and a marketplace for low-cost, third-party plug-ins. For small businesses, the technology problem has largely been solved, leaving only sourcing, fulfillment, and marketing to worry about. Enter the dropship service provider.

For a small business that is interested in either backfilling around a few core products or testing an ecommerce concept without investing significantly into product inventory, dropship can be an excellent partner. It provides a turnkey solution to sourcing, warehousing, and fulfillment of an infinite array of products. The merchant simply sends over the orders to the dropship partner at the end of the day and the dropship provider takes care of the rest.

Companies such as Ordoro and Doba provide a membership program that allows the retail partner to download lists of products that can be easily uploaded into their store for resale. Subscription ecommerce companies even provide a plug-in that directly integrates their product feed into the merchant's. This is a classic example of brokering of products as a service.

Table 6.10 Key attributes and strategies for dropship program

ATTRIBUTES	STRATEGIES
Key partners	Product sourcing
Value proposition	Outsourced supply chain
Key activities	Sourcing, inventory, and fulfillment
Monetization	Membership fee and commission per sale

Subscription

The Subscription Archetype blends the benefits of Product and Service Archetypes and provides its value for an ongoing subscription fee. It has been said that products are too commoditizable and services are not scalable. A way of addressing these issues is to provide a hybrid of the two. This is the case with many of the most innovative businesses of the past decade.

The benefits of a subscription approach to content and software are numerous. Subscription allows implicit financing of what would otherwise be an expensive up-front purchase, thus lowering the barriers to entry for small business and some consumer products. Retaining customers and spreading that revenue over a longer period of time provides more predictable revenue for the business offering the subscription service. And it strikes a meaningful balance between a cost-effective product and the supporting services that actually make it useful for most.

SOFTWARE AS A SERVICE (SAAS)

Software as a Service (SaaS) has become the preferred software development model in the post-Web 2.0 era. Rather than paying a large sum up front to license and download a piece of software, customers can pay a monthly fee to access the hosted version of the software.

For small businesses this presents several new opportunities: first, less cash up front improves cash flow for the business. Second, the headaches of having to install and manage the software in-house are removed. Third, an SaaS model business often provides superior service and support compared to software as a product business.

In many cases, SaaS could be said to be a "productized," lower-cost alternative to what would otherwise require a custom service agency solution. For example, it might cost thousands of dollars to have an agency implement a custom ecommerce system, but SaaS shopping cart providers such as Volusion and BigCommerce now provide hosted basic solutions for $20 per month or less. Provided the merchant is satisfied with the customization limits of the hosting solution, this can be a very efficient solution.

A primary activity of SaaS organizations is software development, since a software product is at the center of the business. It is thus an attractive business model for software engineers seeking to develop a business.

However, SaaS organizations must remember that they are fundamentally service organizations; their product merely automates or adds efficiency to the service, so proactively facilitating customers is a key aspect of their business.

Table 6.11 Key attributes and strategies for SaaS

ATTRIBUTES	STRATEGIES
Key partners	SaaS providers
Value proposition	Turnkey software and management
Key activities	Develop software and manage servers
Monetization	Subscription fee

CONTENT AS A SERVICE (CAAS)

Content as a product is typically sold as a tangible artifact in a market-place, for example, books or e-books being sold on Amazon or songs sold through iTunes. But what about content portals that exist outside of a marketplace and provide ongoing curation of valuable information or insights? This is the Content as a Service (CaaS) prototype.

This type of business may charge a monthly subscription for exclusive content, such as Ancestry.com, or it may monetize its content through advertisement, as is the case with Demand Media and its collection of popular online guide sites. In the case of monthly subscriptions, it is common to offer a free trial period or limited-use option in order to generate actionable leads the company can then market upgrades to. With the advertising model, the content portal might have a number of relationships with various ad networks and may even sell premium ad buys directly to big customers.

Table 6.12 Key attributes and strategies for CaaS

ATTRIBUTES	STRATEGIES
Key partners	CaaS providers
Value proposition	Turnkey software and management
Key activities	Develop software and manage servers
Monetization	Subscription fee

Ecosystem

The Ecosystem Archetype is a hybrid that combines all three primary archetypes (Trade, Product, and Service). It is the holy grail of business models, as it is highly desirable but extremely difficult to achieve. Success of a business in one vertical opens up opportunities to augment the business with additional offerings, each of which adds incremental revenue and reinforces the value of the other revenue streams.

From a strategic perspective, the ecosystem augments the brand's value chain as much as it increases revenue streams every time a synergistic business unit is added. And because the ecosystem is so valuable and so rare, it helps to entrench the brand within its market, providing a highly defensible position. It is simply more valuable to the end-consumer to have the support, resources, and momentum of an entire ecosystem than to purchase a mere commodity. The brand that offers this will stand clearly ahead of the others both in desirability and pricing power.

TECHNOLOGY PLATFORM

Many of the most successful online ecosystems revolve around technology platforms. Apple is a classic example in the consumer space. What started as a set of innovative products became something entirely different when Apple went direct to consumer by opening its own stores. The stores were not just a retail presence that enabled better brokering of their own products. Every store also offered training seminars and a Genius Bar that provided unparalleled support in the computer hardware market.

Overnight the company went from being solely a product business to having a toe in brokering and services as well. Shortly thereafter, the company expanded its burgeoning ecosystem by introducing the App Store, a marketplace for third-party mobile applications. What started as simple computer hardware is a brand now wrapped in a massive value chain that arguably exceeds the value of the commodity itself.

A similar pattern can be seen with companies like Salesforce, Amazon, and Zillow, all of which have core technology platforms that became so popular that the companies were able to offer complimentary services, marketplaces, and networks for third-party businesses to build around.

Table 6.13 Key attributes and strategies for product platform

ATTRIBUTES	STRATEGIES
Key partners	PaaS providers
Value proposition	Turnkey software and management
Key activities	Develop software and manage servers
Monetization	Subscription fee

MEDIA PLATFORM

A content ecosystem is a larger-than-life destination for information and entertainment. This is the classic media portal that Yahoo.com and Google represent. Television networks such as NBC and CBS are examples in the offline world. Social platforms like Facebook and Twitter are further examples of content magnets that give companies tremendous strength of voice for consumer advertising.

These content titans create ecosystems as they monetize their content. All of these companies have their own advertising platforms, and several provide service platforms as well. Facebook, Google, and Twitter in particular have robust APIs that enable other businesses to mash up content or better integrate their ad platforms. These companies also provide a syndicated ad network (Google AdSense in particular) that third-party websites can use to monetize their content by embedding code that calls back to the respective ad platform (**Figure 6.2**).

Table 6.14 Key attributes and strategy for media platform

ATTRIBUTES	STRATEGIES
Key partners	Advertisers
Value proposition	Quality content
Key activities	Content development
Monetization	Advertisement

Business Model Prototypes

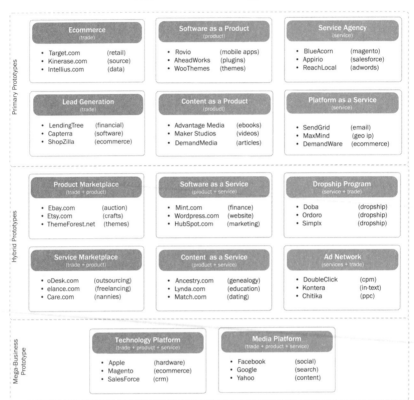

Figure 6.2 Examples for each business model prototype.

Defining your business model

This chapter has covered the seven fundamental business archetypes by introducing a framework that provides a starting point for identifying online business categories. But it is not enough to simply select one of these prototypes. Rather, these serve as a starting point from which to define your own unique model in detail.

In 2010, Alexander Osterwalder introduced a conceptual framework called the Business Model Canvas based on his work on the Business Model Ontology in 2004.[2] With this model there are nine building blocks for creating a well-defined business model, each of which addresses a set of key questions that help to account for the most important parameters of the business (**Figure 6.3**). The purpose of this framework is to provide an accountability matrix to ensure that important attributes such as key partners, customer segments, and applicable channels are considered when developing your model.

It's a good idea to periodically revisit this model as you go through the market-fit stage, and revise your business model specifics, filling out a new template each time you iterate. This discipline will assist you in clarifying the purpose of the iteration and eventually help to crystallize your model along its important criteria.

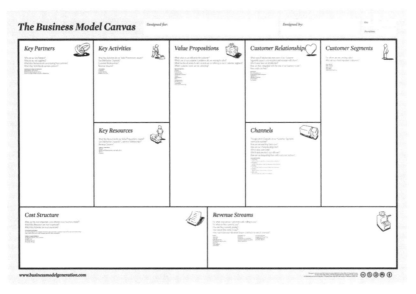

Figure 6.3 The Business Model Canvas.

---

2 http://en.wikipedia.org/wiki/Business_model

Takeaways

- Understand the seven foundational archetypes for online business. Use this foundation to begin planning your own unique buiness model.

- Studying established business models will help you understand businesses similar to what you might develop for your own business.

- Use the Business Model Canvas to develop your own unique business model. It will help you account for important attributes of your business plan.

PART III

DO

CHAPTER 7

SETTING UP YOUR BUSINESS

"I'd rather have one percent of the efforts
of 100 people than 100 percent
of my own efforts."

—J. PAUL GETTY

Already in this book, we've covered a lot of ground. We've decided on
the business vertical that we want to address, and found a viable niche
where we hope to contribute new value and where the competition will
be surmountable. If you have completed all of these steps then congratulations—it's time to start building something!

In the beginning of any new venture there are a few key decisions to consider. One of the biggest is what the team will look like. Should you go
it alone or have a cofounder? Do you have mentors or advisors who can
shepherd you through the process? If you're working with anyone, you'll
need to put together partnership agreements with those individuals.
What should those agreements look like? What's a fair way to compensate those individuals while protecting yourself if they don't contribute
as you'd hoped?

You'll also want to consider how you're going to build your product. Are you going to build it yourself or do you have a technical cofounder? Developing a software product can be expensive. Are you looking at outsourcing or perhaps raising funding to fuel a local team? Have you considered joining a tech accelerator program, which can help you address many of these early issues?

This chapter will address all of these issues and give you an understanding of how to lay a solid foundation to build from.

The hacker and the hustler

Conventional wisdom among the technorati and tech accelerator elite is that any startup needs two to four cofounders to be viable. At a minimum, you need one hacker and one hustler. Steve Jobs and Steve Wozniak are perhaps the most famous example. If you have the luxury of building on that, add a designer and perhaps one additional programmer (**Figure 7.1**).

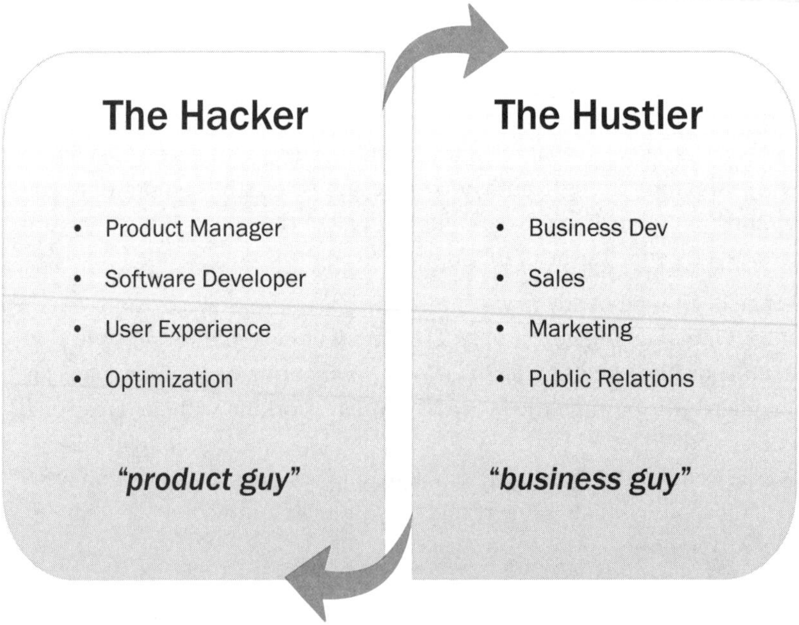

Figure 7.1 The hacker and the hustler.

The hacker in this case is a technical cofounder. He's the programmer who can put things together and can find innovative solutions to meet the near-term business goals. He loves Lean methodology and embraces the art of the "pivot." In most cases, the hacker is not a classically trained software engineer. They favor pragmatic solutions over thoroughly designed enterprise architecture.

The hustler, meanwhile, is all about business development, marketing, and sales. He's probably not an MBA consultant who's mastered supply chain management, but he's excellent at establishing relationships and getting the word out about the product, establishing partnership agreements, and generally creating a buzz.

While this cofounder arrangement seems ideal, it's still a little surprising that most of the tech accelerator programs (Y Combinator, Tech Stars, and so on) won't even consider a single-founder applicant. The logic is that there's so much to be done that a single person can't possibly accomplish it all in a reasonable amount of time, or risk the window of opportunity passing him by. Perhaps equally important, it's very difficult for someone to switch back and forth between "heads up" and "heads down" tasks. To develop a quality product, a hacker needs the opportunity to focus on small details without interruption. As he focuses on the details, he tends to avoid phone calls and meetings and become obsessed with completing the product. But this is toxic to relationship building, sales, and marketing. So even if someone believes he possesses the skills to do both, the context switching is just too much of a burden and should be avoided.

While it may not be necessary to find a cofounder if you're not seeking funding or accelerator support, it's worth pondering this point for a little while if it's considered so important by the accelerators. Perhaps you're a software engineer by day and a hacker of your own product by night, but you have no cofounder and would rather not have one. Perhaps you should consider other creative ways to enlist business and marketing support. Think about setting up an aggressive affiliate marketing program and recruit top super affiliates to promote your product for you.

There are many ways to structure a solution, but the key point here is that it's tough to be both technical and business-focused at the same time and still be effective, so you'll need to find a solution that's workable in your own situation.

Incorporating your startup

It is important to consider the legal entity you want to conduct business under. The decisions you make here will have tax and legal liability implications and will affect how you structure partnerships later. The benefits of a formal corporate structure are not without added cost and complexity, however, so it's important to consider carefully.

Many young startups elect to postpone formal incorporation during the early stages, prior to going to market with their product or service. This is because of the cost and complexity of maintaining a corporate entity. There are numerous filings required throughout the year, such as quarterly tax filings and stock declarations that you must stay on top of, or face penalties and interest if missed. There are additional fees as well. In the state of California, for example, there's an annual minimum of $800 that must be paid each year, regardless of income. This can be an undue burden on a young startup that's not yet generating significant income to reach that threshold of tax liability. Taxes are also much more complex with a corporate entity and you could easily find that you're paying a couple thousand dollars per year for an accountant to file your taxes, rather than a couple hundred, which you might otherwise pay for a standard personal filing.

While it may be reasonable to do your research and build the prototype without a formal corporate entity, once you begin interacting with the outside world on behalf of your new venture, it's probably time to set up a formal corporate entity. Signing agreements, entering into partnership, and comingling personal and business funds all open you up to liabilities that you must be mindful of. Even providing a service and accepting payment may have potential tax and legal liability implications.

Another important consideration when delaying incorporation is your ability to establish credit and a record of doing business. It may not seem like a significant issue now, but if you anticipate needing to take loans on behalf of your business, you'll want to establish a bank account, get a credit card, and register your business with Dun & Bradstreet as early as possible. Most startups won't be able to get a loan until they've been in business for two to three years, so it will help to plan ahead in this regard. Certain professional organizations such as the Better Business Bureau (BBB) also will not list companies until they've been in business for a year or more.

If you're ready to file your corporate entity, there are a number of options to get started. Traditionally, a founder would ask his lawyer or accountant to advise him and file the appropriate paperwork; if you have the budget, it is certainly advisable to do so. There are, after all, a number of liability and tax planning considerations that go into deciding the appropriate entity type (LLC, S Corp, C Corp) and location in which to incorporate (local, Delaware, and so on). Because of the considerable cost savings, however, it's becoming increasingly popular for those with straightforward incorporation needs to use specialized service firms such as the Company Corporation, RocketLawyer, or LegalZoom, which can help you understand the options and prepare filings at a significantly lower cost.

The advisor

An advisor can be an invaluable resource as you build your new business, particularly one aligned with a specific aspect of your business in which you might be a bit weak. In many cases the advisor can be a mentor to you or your team. This is someone with seniority who has traveled the same path you're currently on and who can provide critical insights to help you avoid the most painful lessons and mistakes along the way.

In other cases, though, the advisor might be a domain expert who possesses specific business domain knowledge that you or your team do not. For example, let's say that you've determined you'll create a software as a service (SaaS) product to service the practice management needs of dentists. You're an excellent software engineer and your business-development partner (the hustler) may even have had experience selling in the dental market segment in the past.

But what do you really know about the practice of dentistry or creating ideal workflows for the profession? And how will you create a compelling product that resonates with your target audience if you can't speak to these nuances? In this case, you might consider finding a practicing dentist who can advise you in the early stages of product design and provide feedback during later iterations to perfect the user experience.

Finding an advisor

In the past, entrepreneurship mentors were hard to come by and most people relied on traditional networks. A mentor was someone you happened to know already through friend and family connections, a professor in the local university, or a fellow member of a professional organization or society such as Rotary. But today tech accelerator programs and co-working destinations are quickly becoming the conduit of choice for connecting young entrepreneurs with established entrepreneurs with Internet-specific knowledge.

Domain knowledge experts still require a more organic approach to networking but are often not as hard to find. You might be surprised how easy it is to find an entrepreneurially minded professional who wouldn't mind advising you on your startup project. After all, it costs the advisor little but provides some financial upside as well as some status of being a thought leader in the industry. Consider looking for professional organizations that cater to your specific industry of interest, or attend local Chamber of Commerce meetings to make those connections.

Compensating the advisor

Neither the mentor nor the domain expert advisor is an active member of your core team, but their contributions are still quite valuable and you want to respect that, so how do you compensate them? Because this has become such a common dilemma, the Founder Institute, a tech accelerator program, has created a standardized advisor agreement (FAST) and made it publicly available.[1] It provides an equity compensation schedule between 0.25 and 1.0 percent of total equity, based on the level of expertise and stage of the contribution (how early in the process). The FAST agreement has been well received by the startup community and appears to be a fair and reasonable approach to advisor compensation.

---

1 http://fi.co/contents/FAST (Founder Advisor Standard Template)

Partnership agreements

If you're going to have partners, you need a written agreement from the very beginning. Some of the biggest disputes among partners come about as a result of misunderstandings or disagreements over expectations, contributions, and ownership. If you find it an uncomfortable topic now, then there's a good chance that the parties are already not on the same page and you're setting yourself up for problems later. Even if it dampens some of the enthusiasm, it's an important conversation that you need to have with your partners at the start and the agreement needs to be put in writing. This lays a solid foundation for fairness, transparency, and better communication.

Should you see a lawyer to draft the partnership agreement in the beginning? Of course it's ideal to rely upon a legal professional for any legal document, but it's not a legal requirement for a binding agreement. You must balance this preference against the financial limitations and priorities of the business early on. What is most important is to get the key principles of your partnership on paper and to have all parties sign the agreement. And while an attorney can certainly help you to ensure that the important points of the agreement are accounted for, there are alternative resources online that can also assist with this goal for those on a tighter budget.

Let's look at the key issues you'll need to consider and account for.

Identify partnership

You must clearly identify the partnership to which the agreement will apply. If you have formed a corporation, LLC, or partnership entity, that entity will be identified, typically at the top of the document.

Roles and contributions

Each partner must be clearly identified and his role and contributions clearly identified. For example, if one cofounder will be contributing a specified amount of cash or property and the other will be managing day-to-day operations and thus contributing his time, state this clearly.

State any specific articles of property, exact amounts of cash, and time. In the case of time, consider specifying the value of time, based on the opportunity cost of foregone employment. For example, if the managing founder expects to forego six months of employment at an opportunity cost of $50,000, specify this cost as a contribution and attach a dollar value to it. Without specifying the value of the contribution, it's difficult to normalize and compare time versus financial or property contributions.

Expectations and duties

The partnership is fundamentally an investment and should be acknowledged as such. If a partner contributes cash, property, or time, there is an implicit expectation of a return on that investment. This is your opportunity to make that implicit expectation an explicit one. Discuss with your partners and be specific about exactly what is expected from the investment. Who is the CEO? Are decisions to be taken as a group, or will a dominant partner make day-to-day decisions? Is a minimum time commitment expected, or additional cash or property promised upon completion of a specific phase or as needed?

Compensation

What sort of compensation will be due each partner and on what schedule? It's typical for a startup to have no profits to distribute in the beginning. But what about living stipends? And how will profits be distributed later, and based on what event will profit distributions begin? For example, you might specify that based on an initial investment, each partner foregoing employment is entitled to a $2,000 per month living stipend. Perhaps 50 percent of profits will be distributed after the second quarter of positive cash flow is achieved, while the other 50 percent will be reinvested into business growth. A cash or property investor may also prefer to have that investment paid back prior to any profit distributions and that should be spelled out if so.

Vesting

One of the most common and difficult issues is a partner who initially commits a specific amount of time per month, but whose priorities and commitment change over time. If you don't account for this issue, a partner could be entitled to a large percentage of your business based on an incomplete agreement that does not temper that entitlement based on performance. To solve this, consider implementing a vesting schedule. It's common for companies to require a four- to five-year vesting period in which no equity (or profits) is distributed during the first year of the partnership. Equity (and implicitly profit entitlements) is then distributed gradually each year, based upon continued fulfillment of duties, until the completion of the fifth year, at which point the partner has vested and is entitled to full equity and profits, as per the agreement.

Liquidation

What happens if a partner chooses to leave the partnership? Let's say, for example, the partner has completed his five-year vesting term and is thus a full partner. If he leaves, is he entitled to a full cash liquidation of his equity stake in the business? Can he sell his stake or is he required to provide a first option of purchase to the partnership as a buy-back before seeking purchase or other liquidation opportunities outside the partnership? It may be best for the partnership to require a first-right option to purchase back the equity as an entity but, ultimately, this is up to the members of the partnership to decide.

Admitting new partners

Many startups will need to either raise investment capital or take on strategic partners along the way to augment their efforts. How will the partnership allocate additional equity to provide for this new partner? Will it be an equal dilution of all partners or are early property and cash investors preferred equity holders, while only the time investors are diluted? It actually may be difficult to anticipate all such details and you may need the investment capital enough that you're willing to revise these terms when you get to that point, but it's good to start with an agreed default plan among the partners. You can make amendments later as needed.

Complete contract

Finally, you'll want to state that the contract is a "complete and severable" agreement. The contract should be stated as complete, meaning there are no other agreements or that if agreements do exist, this agreement shall supersede any prior agreements and override the terms that may have existed in any such prior agreements.

Should you outsource?

At a high level, outsourcing simply means sourcing a solution from an external party. In the world of software development, however, it typically means offshoring development of your software product to a lower-cost country. This can provide a myriad of benefits to a small business. It can mean real-time team augmentation without the long-term commitment of hiring someone. And by realizing one of the greatest benefits of the Internet, social connectedness, it's relatively easy to source experienced engineers with specific technical knowledge that you might require for your project. Sites like oDesk.com and Freelancer.com provide the ability to search freelancers and even dedicated agencies around the world based on skill, fees, availability, and even their reputation within that specific online community.

But the biggest opportunity that outsourcing appears to provide for startups is the ability to source product development at a fraction of the cost of having a local team. It's not uncommon to find experienced engineers in countries such as India or the Philippines who bill several multiples less per hour than their American counterparts.

On the surface this seems to be a huge opportunity for a startup, with many compelling upsides. And that can sometimes be the case. But more often than not, there are costs and inefficiencies that creep into the equation that cause outsourcing to be less desirable than it first appears. For an experienced software engineer or product manager who is able to effectively manage a longer and more complex supply chain, outsourcing can still be a viable option that provides incremental value compared to the cost of running your own team. But the benefit is not nearly as big as it first seems.

Here are just a few of the challenges to anticipate when outsourcing:

1. Communication

   The challenges of communicating with a developer or a team of developers in a different time zone and culture, who may not be native speakers of your language, cannot be overstated. The differences in time zone can mean that a simple response on a small issue may get volleyed back and forth over several days due to asynchronous communication, rather than getting resolved in a single conversation. Differences in culture can be a real challenge as well. Developers in the Western world are often accountable for their deliverables and will fill in the gaps when insufficient communication occurs, while in other countries work may stop if such gaps in direction occur.

2. Methodology

   It's difficult to practice small-batch iterative development (Agile/Lean) due to the communication issues. For this and a myriad of other reasons it's best to work on a fixed-cost basis when outsourcing development, which means using Waterfall methodology. For better or worse, you need to plan to spend considerable up-front time to plan out your project and thoroughly document every detail of it before starting that phase of development. This is your best opportunity to avoid the communication problems that can otherwise occur. Since iterative process is better for product/market-fit discovery, this also has inefficiency implications and suggests why outsourcing may be a better fit, once product-market fit has been validated.

3. Quality of work

   Quality of code is a persistent problem in outsourced projects that has been expressed by many companies that have utilized offshore resources. The challenge seems to directly correlate with the cost of labor in that region. Expect that you will face the biggest challenges with quality from the same geographic regions where you find the best rates. In our own experience, we were quite surprised to see the naïve and in some cases outright neglectful errors in the code we received.

There could be many reasons for these phenomena. It could be cultural expectations or perhaps it's simply the lack of accountability to an otherwise anonymous client. Whatever the case, it's a manageable nuisance for a seasoned engineer or product manager, but something that can absolutely sink a project for a client who is less technically equipped to manage the process.

What is the right decision?

Outsourcing provides many cost and team augmentation advantages that are worth considering as an early-stage startup, but it's not the profound opportunity it may first seem and is generally not the best long-term option for a startup built around the success of a software product. The pros and cons must be weighed carefully. Development turnaround generally takes longer, quality and communications can be a struggle, Lean method discovery does not work as well, and the process often requires significantly more management overhead. By the time you factor in all of these inefficiencies, the typical offshore project is only marginally more cost effective than working with a local team that takes ownership over the long-term outcome of the product.

Should you seek investment capital?

The decision of whether to raise capital for your business can be a complex one and there is no uniform correct answer. You must weigh the costs and the advantages for your unique business. First and foremost, ask yourself whether it's really necessary for your business plan. The cost of launching an online product has fallen precipitously in the past 10 years and the cost of starting a business is now arguably the lowest it has ever been (**Figure 7.2**). Angel investor and investment partner Mark Suster pointed out that what once would have cost $5 million to launch can now be done for under $5,000.[2]

---

2 http://www.slideshare.net/benoitwirz/community-foundation-startup-presentation

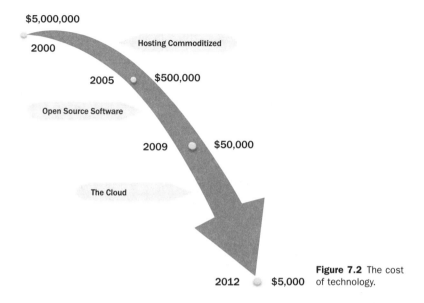

Figure 7.2 The cost of technology.

Despite these low development costs, the competitive reality does often necessitate capital. We are no longer in the early stages of the Internet and in just about any direction you might look to compete, you'll find numerous competitors, several of which may have raised considerable money. Even if you're able to launch your initial product without the money, you need to be pragmatic about whether you can compete for mindshare in your market without a significant marketing budget, and without the funds to compete on advanced features as time progresses.

There are downsides, too. Less than 10 percent of all companies that seek funding will actually receive it. According to AngelSoft, your odds of successfully raising funding are less than your odds of writing a *New York Times* best-selling book![3] You can spend considerable time chasing investors and raising capital; imagine how far you could have progressed your product by spending those same three to six months on product development or marketing instead.

---

3 http://www.openforum.com/idea-hub/topics/money/article/
   how-to-raise-money-when-nobody-is-investing-1/

Another issue to consider is that any investment money you take is typically on a preferred stock basis, meaning that if you ever must liquidate your business, the investors get paid back in full before you see a dime. Given the lower odds of success among higher-stakes investment-backed startups, there's a good chance that you'll walk away with nothing. You also can lose control of the direction and perhaps even day-to-day operations of your company, depending how much capital you raise, relative to your valuation.

If you decide to raise capital, consider whether you fit the profile of what most angels and venture capitalists are seeking. You absolutely must have a team, preferably of the hacker and hustler configuration. You must be working on a product or automated service or trade solution; traditional services companies are generally considered unscalable and will not be funded. You're at a strong disadvantage if you're not located in one of the major software centers. Your investors will prefer that you are in their regional market, and a large majority of Internet investors are based in Silicon Valley, with secondary pockets in other tech hotspots such as Seattle, Boston, New York, and Los Angeles.

Some startups decide to self-fund through other means such as consulting income. A service business such as consulting or agency work can serve as an excellent springboard for launching products, since client work can pay your living expenses and provide excess working capital to fund your ventures. And with a little advance tax planning, you may even be able to defer taxes on those product investments.

In the final analysis, having capital can be a significant strategic advantage when you consider how much money is already in the market and how advanced existing products and competitors already are. Unless there's something inherently viral or profound about your product, there's a good chance that you'll face an uphill battle while trying to gain traction, and having the resources to push you along could mean the difference between success or failure. But be realistic about your need for capital and your likelihood of successfully raising it, as the path of fundraising can be a significant distraction.

Startup accelerators

In 2005, Paul Graham founded Y Combinator, a new startup investment model that brought young startups into a three-month mentorship
program, provided each founder with an $18,000 living stipend, and pro-
vided one-on-one mentorship and classes on entrepreneurship. At the
end of the program, the company holds Demo Day, where all of the startups from that cohort present their products in science fair style. Investors
from around the area are invited to tour the product demos and a handful of the founders walk away with capital to fuel further development of
their product. Since 2005, Y Combinator has helped launch hundreds
of startups, including Airbnb, Reddit, Loopt, Scribd, and Dropbox.[4]

Since the introduction of Y Combinator, tech accelerators have popped
up all over the United States. There are a few other well-known programs
such as TechStars in Boulder and Seattle, AngelPad in San Francisco,
and the Launch Pad in Los Angeles. Y Combinator, however, is still the
most famous and well regarded of the accelerators. With more than 4,000
applications each semester, the program is able to accept only the top
1 percent of total applicants.

These programs are often billed as the alternative to an MBA for those
who are interested primarily in starting a business. They are geared
toward young tech-savvy entrepreneurs who are near the end of college
or who have recently graduated. For young entrepreneurs, this is a fantastic opportunity to learn about business, receive mentorship from noted
tech entrepreneurs, and establish a professional network that will help
them in their entrepreneurial pursuits down the road. And even for those
who don't ultimately receive funding, the program cost them nothing,
took only a few months of their time, and provided a prestigious resume
line item that will help them get a great job at another startup.

For investors, the tech accelerator itself is quite an innovation. Whereas
investment firms once had to commit larger amounts of capital to one
startup versus another, they now have a vehicle by which to invest a small
amount of capital into 40 to 50 companies at a time. Each participating
company issues 5 to 7 percent stock warrants to the tech accelerator in
return for the training and early funding they receive. And because these

4 http://ycombinator.com/

programs attract so much attention, they're able to pick the best of the best as participants. Now the same investment capital is spread over about 40 to 50 solid early-stage startups and because of this diffusion of risk, the odds of positive ROI for each lump investment are higher. Essentially, investors get the same or better return on investment but at a much lower risk. This is why tech accelerators are popping up in every major market.

This is an important dynamic to evaluate when considering a tech accelerator program. Because accelerators are playing the spread, so to speak, they are incentivized to encourage and invest in higher-stakes businesses. They are invested in enough young startups to cover their spread. But what is in the best interest of the fund may not be in the best interest of the individual startup. Consider whether you're personally interested in a game-changing business, or prefer something less high profile but with higher odds of success. Are you looking to change the World, or simply create a lifestyle business?

A tech accelerator can be an excellent vehicle by which to launch your online startup and perhaps your entrepreneurship career if you fit the profile and can get accepted. The extensive network connections, access to capital, and mentorship opportunities can kick your efforts into hyperdrive. But you generally need to be working on a higher-stakes business proposition, must have a cofounder (preferably of the hacker and hustler configuration), and should be young and able to put your life on hold for a completely immersive experience.

Takeaways

- It's generally better to have a cofounder than to develop a business on your own. The cofounder should be skilled at different aspects of the business than you are.

- Advisors can help you avoid pitfalls and suggest opportunities for efficiency. The FAST agreement provides a standard agreement to compensate advisors for their mentorship.

- Raising investment funds can have a significant impact on your ability to compete or develop a product, but it's not without its own cost and complexity. Be pragmatic about whether capital is needed to viably compete in your market.

CHAPTER 8

DEVELOPING YOUR PRODUCT

"Ideas are easy. Implementation is hard."

—GUY KAWASAKI, COFOUNDER, ALLTOP

In this chapter we'll discuss effective strategies and decisions for developing your first working prototype. The goal at this point is to find a pragmatic balance between building a product that will grow to a reasonable level and respond easily to rapid learning and changes in business concept.

Because this is your initial prototype you have to expect that changes to your product will come quickly based on user feedback, and may send the product in a very different direction, within a short period of time. This means there's a good chance your code will be a mess by the time you find market fit, and before you begin to realize serious scale demands on your software.

It's understandably tempting for a good software developer to want to develop everything the "right way," using the latest technology frameworks and rigorous and scalable architectures, but consider that this goes against the primary stated goals at this stage of keeping costs low and responding quickly to user feedback, that may send your product in different directions. The justification for creating rigorous architectural constructs is cleaner code and less work or bugs later. But what if those constructs cost more now and never get used later? Or worse, what if they actually create more scaffolding that you have to undo later, when you realize your fundamental product assumptions were wrong?

For all of these reasons, we advocate taking a *hacker* approach to developing your initial product or prototype. In other words, don't use complicated frameworks and don't worry about writing overly efficient code; just focus on putting together a reasonable user experience and getting it out the door so the hustler on your team can begin testing and validating the market. This refers back to the discussion about the hacker and hustler team we described in the previous chapter. Take a pragmatic perspective, not one of an idealist or a skilled artisan. These ideals contradict our stated goals at this stage of the process.

With this perspective in mind, let's discuss building your initial product (prototype).

The Lean Method

A movement called Lean methodology has been spreading among Internet startups and throughout Silicon Valley as a whole. It aims to solve the problem that plagues most startups—how to reduce risk and more systematically arrive at a product that customers will pay for. By following Lean practices, a startup can maximize the odds of success and reduce what's at stake if the company fails, making it possible to try again later.

First a little background: Lean manufacturing is a process originally developed by John Krafcik and published in a paper titled *Triumph of the Lean Production System* in 1988. The name comes from the idea of "thinning warehouse inventory" to only what's necessary for current work in progress, thus improving efficiency. The concepts were later applied at Toyota along with concurrent development of concepts such as Flow and Just in Time (JIT). These concepts were subsequently studied and applied by Steve Blank at Stanford and by Blank's student, Eric Ries, to the Internet startup movement, reflecting his experiences with a startup and the needs of a process while working in venture capital at Kleiner Perkins.

The principal issue that most startups struggle with is discovering product-market fit. And thus the focus of Lean methodology within a startup is to systematically discover what customers will pay for, as quickly as possible, reducing development and marketing cost (**Figure 8.1**). To solve these problems, practitioners of Lean process focus on the creation of a minimum viable product (MVP, a term coined by Marc Andreessen) and on a continuous iterative method of testing and refining the product. Test early, and test often. If you create a simple prototype, get it in front of target customers early, then revise or "pivot" in a new direction as needed, you won't waste the next two years developing the perfect product that no one wanted.

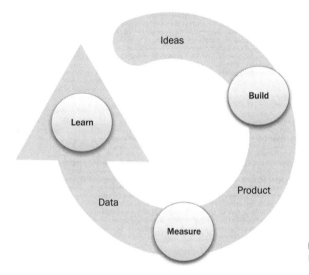

Figure 8.1
Lean methodology.

There is an assumption with Lean that the problem with traditional manufacturing methodology is batch size. Henry Ford's assembly line was a revolution that led to mass manufacturing, and it is massively efficient, if you assume nothing is wrong. But when something does go wrong, this approach can lead to catastrophic results. And when you're in a highly unpredictable environment such as an Internet startup, this only increases the risk of a negative outcome.

The solution is to use smaller batch sizes with a tight Build > Measure > Learn > feedback loop that minimizes mistakes and offers course correction along the way. Larger batch sizes may be appropriate in some cases down the road, though certainly not in an early-stage startup.

Three core values of the Lean manufacturing process are still reflected in
modern adaptations of the Lean startup method:

1. Challenge

   Challenge your beliefs and assumptions. Don't allow yourself to
   believe that you know what will work best. Empirical testing often
   disproves the assumptions of even the best expert!

2. Kaizen

   Continuous improvement is part of the daily process. There's never
   a "good enough." Seeking improvement should be a part of the process every day.

3. Genchi Genbutsu

   Loosely translated, this means "go see for yourself" Or as Steve
   Blank says, "There are no facts inside your building. So get the heck
   outside your building and go find the facts."[1] You must engage with
   customers as part of the building process, and see how they use
   your product, to look for opportunities to improve.

The fundamental goal behind all three of these methods is responsive
product design, which builds on customer feedback to more quickly
find product-market fit by better integrating customer input into the
design process. This goal is accomplished by building your product in
small-batch iterations and putting those releases in front of prospective
customers for feedback that will drive the planning of further iterations.

Wireframe prototyping

One of the best ways to facilitate this process is with wireframe prototyping (**Figure 8.2**). Using a tool such as Axure or Balsamiq, it's possible
to create a series of wireframe diagrams that demonstrate what a set
of pages would look like. You can then hyperlink buttons and regions
of those wireframes and link to them together, allowing users to click
through them and experience page flow as if they were clicking through
an actual website.

---

1 Steve Blank (2005), *Four Steps to the Epiphany: Successful Strategies for Products
that Win* CafePress.com

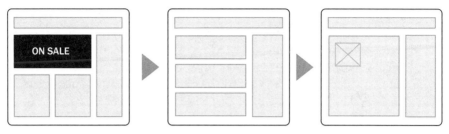

Figure 8.2 Clickable wireframe prototyping.

While it may seem like an extra step to create this prototype, the time investment will easily pay for itself compared to going through the same process with actual code. Imagine the profound time savings of simply drawing a few boxes and linking them together for prototype review, rather than having to prepare images, create HTML, CSS, JavaScript, and back-end code to actually implement the scenario just to get the same input. Now imagine performing these steps repeatedly as you work with your customers to arrive at product-market fit, and you'll quickly realize the value of this approach.

At a high level, Lean is not complicated, but for anyone experienced in traditional Waterfall production methods, this can be a powerful concept that turns things upside down. Getting started and applying these principles need not be hard either; it's really just about shifting the focus away from a supply-driven mindset in which you focus on what you're building and shifting toward demand-driven production, in which you focus more on listening and responding to the needs and desires of your customer.

Choosing a technology platform

Choosing the right technology platform on which to build your online presence depends on many factors. If you're just getting started and your primary concern is building a prototype, you'll have very different criteria compared to someone who has already raised capital and is looking to build a scalable product.

If you're a technologist, you're no doubt tuned in to the hot technologies of the moment and are probably looking for an opportunity to leverage them. After all, leveraging those technologies is more interesting, it reinforces your skilled profession, and it may even have an added benefit of the respect of some tech-centric investors, particularly in places like Silicon Valley. But don't put the cart before the horse!

Remember that the primary goals for the moment are finding product-market fit as quickly as possible and spending as little money as reasonable in the process. In fact, there's a business management model that supports this prioritization. Robert Kaplan and David Norton's Balanced Scorecard method acknowledges the tendency of businesses to emphasize certain goals over others, which can cause long-term imbalances and dysfunctions within an organization (**Figure 8.3**).[2] The Balanced Scorecard provides a more holistic and pragmatic approach to setting the priorities of the organization.

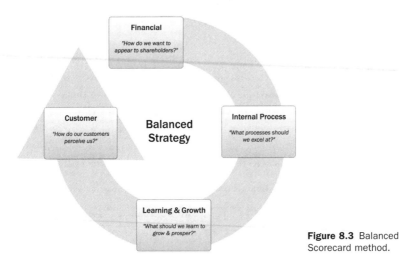

Figure 8.3 Balanced Scorecard method.

---

2 Kaplan R S and Norton D P (1996) "Balanced Scorecard: Translating Strategy into Action" Harvard Business School Press

In the conceptual framework of Balanced Scorecard, objectives, key performance measures, targets, and initiatives are exposed and compared along the lines of financial, customer, business process, and learning and growth criteria using a chart such as this one:

	OBJECTIVES	MEASURES	TARGETS	INITIATIVES
FINANCIAL				
CUSTOMER				
PROCESS				
LEARNING				

Using this framework, an organization will be better prepared to prioritize and make decisions by looking at the whole impact of a given initiative, at the expense of other objectives.

So consider the current state of your startup and whether you can justify spending the time to ramp up and support the latest technologies rather than building a user experience quickly and focusing on measuring user experience. That would be prioritizing the future state of the business process ahead of the immediate viability of your startup.

Provided that you're successful in eventually finding product-market fit, you will surely have the opportunity to explore the myriad of frameworks and technologies. By that point the product will likely have pivoted a few times, the logic you've written will be a mess, and it will be time to step back and rebuild the application the right way anyway. In the meantime, consider using a loosely structured approach that's easy to start with, easy to hack through, and easy to find talent to help you with. Keep your prototyping hat on for the moment and focus on selecting a technology that will let you quickly and cheaply iterate and pivot until your model is well defined.

Cost expectations

It's important to note that as a startup you are a product, a process, or both—that costs money, either explicitly or implicitly (opportunity cost). Nontechnical founders are often surprised to learn that creating a sophisticated product can cost into the tens of thousands of dollars. Technical founders meanwhile are often surprised at how much time and marketing goes into developing a client or customer base.

Expectations mismatch

The availability of open source platforms and lower-cost solutions is a great thing for innovation and for consumers, but it creates cost expectations that are often unrealistic when you begin to look at developing custom software products. As businesses go deeper into custom work, there are fewer templates and fewer frameworks and technology stacks on which they can stand to accomplish their task. As a result, costs and time requirements will begin to scale exponentially. There is, after all, a reason why Amazon.com spends millions of dollars each year to employ hundreds of engineers and yet you can have your own ecommerce site for $20 per month.

This dichotomy seems to always be an issue for the nontechnical entrepreneur to accept. The same issue is observable among midsize businesses when a nontechnical manager looks into deeper system integration. This issue is one of perceived value, since open source software and free-to-use online solutions have anchored cost expectations for technology very low. It created an unrealistic cost expectation for developing new technology (**Figure 8.4**).

This mismatch of expectations is most pronounced with those who are close to the top of the value/cost/time pyramid. If you're only accustomed to interacting with technology at a consumer level, remember that this is where the greatest commoditization has occurred and the least amount of customization is provided. Conversely, each layer deeper into the value pyramid will yield greater competitive differentiation, but at exponentially higher cost, due to the cost of discovering and developing this technology.

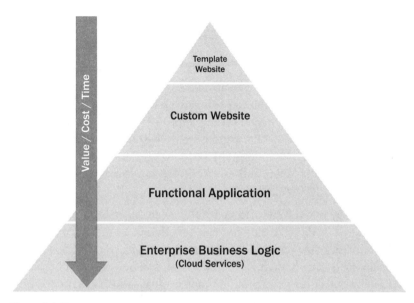

Figure 8.4 The value pyramid.

This is why the SaaS business model is so meaningful for consumers and why so many startups have embraced this business model. It promises to make available solutions that have real value for individuals or smaller businesses that couldn't afford them before. It democratizes technology that was previously available only to elite organizations by better diffusing cost. But that doesn't mean the cost of development doesn't exist.

Now that we've established why custom software development costs are high, we'll spend the balance of the chapter discussing effective methods for developing the product while keeping costs low.

When code should suck

There's a fundamental difference between a software engineer and a hacker. A software engineer typically has a degree in computer science. He has studied and values proper software architecture and design patterns as much if not more than the outcome; this is the true software artisan. A hacker on the other hand is typically someone who is self-taught and who learned to program for the sake of accomplishing a task. He may have progressed to substantial skill in software engineering, but is still a pragmatist with the end goal in mind.

You'll typically find formally trained software engineers working for large software organizations to either create new software products or perform systems integrations on large enterprise applications. They place high value on the quality of their work. A good software engineer will prefer working in object-oriented programming languages such as Java or Ruby, and will insist on using an MVC framework, ORM utilities, test-driven development (TDD), and a host of other scaffolding that will result in a robust and sustainable application. A hacker on the other hand will find the cheapest and quickest way to accomplish a task, and generally will prefer simple scripting languages or rapid development platforms, without the weight of the additional scaffolding.

What a startup needs in the earliest stages of development is a hacker, not a software engineer. The hacker can better balance the business objectives and will be less tied to best-practice constructs that slow down the MVP and subsequent pivots and iterations.

Sometimes pivoting means going in a completely different direction than you first anticipated. In cases like this, scaffolding is just more *stuff* to undo; it adds to the time and cost of pivoting, and it leaves more of a mess in its wake, increasing bugs, and so on. All the goals that the framework facilitates manifest the exact opposite conditions if applied to an early startup context. For this reason, it's not only perfectly acceptable to write that taboo spaghetti code that every good engineer knows to avoid, it's actually preferable in the earliest stages of prototyping. You can go back and write things the "right way" later, once you've established your business model and have the cash flow or investment capital to justify it.

Agile vs. Waterfall

If you're a software developer or have talked to one recently, you've probably heard about the wonders of Agile development. This is likely the best process if you're working with a small team of local developers, but it may not be appropriate if you've outsourced your development effort, particularly overseas. To crystallize this point and to fully cover the product development process, let's review Agile and Waterfall methodologies.

Iterative methodology (Agile)

Iterative methods such as Scrum, Extreme Programming, and the Rational Unified Process (RUP) rose to prominence in the 1990s, in response to the perceived shortcomings of Waterfall and other sequential approaches. In 2001, the Agile Manifesto was written to unify these efforts and the Agile method was born. Traditional sequential approaches such as Waterfall are great for reducing the cost of production, but they're slow to produce results (since planning must be completed before implementation begins) and outright terrible at discovery and responding to user feedback. Proponents of iterative methods argue that while the Waterfall makes efficient use of capital and resources to develop a known outcome, they're only efficient in creating something that nobody wants, when applied to early-stage product development, in which discovery is still a critical issue.

Generally compatible with the Lean philosophy of product development, the Agile method focuses on software development and includes several subprocesses such as Scrum, Extreme Programming, and Adaptive (**Figure 8.5**). Collectively, they provide tactical guidance and frameworks for implementing iterative development processes within an organization. The Scrum subprocess, for example, emphasizes face-to-face communication and requires a daily meeting between team members to provide updates and social accountability, as well as to align everyone around the common goals and challenges. It also recommends that all members of the team work together in a single office without walls (called a "bull pen") to facilitate open and organic communication. The idea is that the team can be more reactive and ultimately agile and responsive to changing business requirements this way.

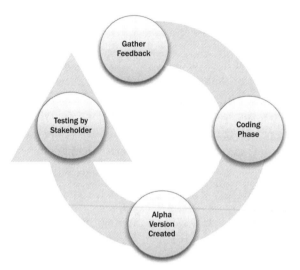

Figure 8.5
Agile development.

Agile also mandates that delegates from each business unit be an active part of the process, every step of the way. Each iteration is typically a two- to six-week timebox. While developers are implementing the design for the current iteration, designers and business stakeholders are creating the requirements for the next iteration, to be completed at the same time as the implementation of the current one. When the current implementation is completed, it goes to QA to test while development works on the next iteration, and so forth.

In this way, design and functional requirements are being created shortly before they're implemented. This allows for a tight feedback loop in which product designers quickly realize flaws in implementation and business stakeholders can quickly perform user testing and correct any flawed assumptions about what's actually being built.

The Lean method is similar to the Agile method as it is iterative in nature, though the focus is product-market fit, not product implementation. Agile provides a feedback loop for internal discovery among business units; Lean focuses on customer feedback, discovering product-market fit, and optimization details such as conversion rate and landing page optimization.

Sequential design process (Waterfall)

Sequential design processes such as Waterfall emphasize completion of one task before proceeding to the next (**Figure 8.6**). For example, a business stakeholder must perform due diligence and complete requirements documentation before passing the project to the technology leads to perform technical analysis and the designers to implement a graphic design. Upon completion of the technical analysis and graphic design artifacts, the project is ready to be implemented by programmers.

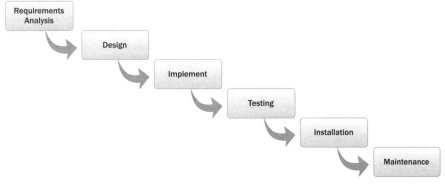

Figure 8.6 Waterfall methodology.

This approach has some benefits. The business team is forced to gather all of its requirements before production begins and that can be a fantastic incentive to get the business stakeholders to prioritize the effort and complete the document. Otherwise, business stakeholders might be inclined to do a half effort, pass along a requirements document lacking details, and expect technologists to begin designing and building the product, causing the entire effort to produce an unsatisfactory outcome.

Waterfall can also be a significant advantage from a budgeting perspective. When working with external vendors or even service units within a larger enterprise, all of which are driven by strict annual budgeting, there can be little tolerance for wasting money. By practicing a Waterfall methodology, business stakeholders get everything in place to be maximally efficient with the use of technology and design resources before engaging them, thereby reducing capital waste. And, the vendor can also deliver on a fixed cost or fixed timeline, which helps overcome trust issues that can be a problem when working with external vendors who bill by the hour.

Comparison

So which is a better option for your organization? It depends. Waterfall has been beaten up a lot by those who reject it in favor of iteration, but it's actually a better fit when working with external vendors, since cost control is often a key issue. Agile can be a great choice within organizations that are customer focused and that foster an open environment for communication and interdepartmental cooperation. However, many organizations lack the kind of culture needed to succeed with Agile.

The nature of the project is also important. If you're working on creative or discovery-driven projects such as analytics-driven optimization[3] or are simply charged with increasing revenue by whatever means, iteration is the only option, since you need to make changes, test, and respond systematically. Conversely, if you're performing a system integration project with very specific requirements that aren't going to change and require no discovery, Waterfall will likely bring you more success.

Another consideration is the composition of your team. Agile is often preferred among big-picture and senior members of a team who have the competence and awareness of overall business objectives to be effective. It's good to engage such people and give them the opportunity to work with Agile and Lean methods, since they're likely to get bored and not be challenged by having every detail spelled out to them in a Waterfall-style requirements document. Conversely, junior team members often need the structure and oversight of a more structured environment and might not perform well on an Agile team. Agile has also been implicated as noneffective on larger teams. If you have more than 20 people on your project team, managing rapid-succession iterations might overwhelm your effort.

Finally, consider stepping back from all of the details of what sequential and iterative methodologies are and simply ask yourself this question: Does your business benefit more from a large-batch or small-batch approach; discovery or cost control? Sequential Waterfall process is much like an assembly line—it assumes you have all the answers and aren't making any strategy mistakes. It requires up-front planning and is slower with customer response loops but better at controlling costs and accounting for a less-skilled development team. If you're an early-stage

---

3 http://enlogica.com/about/process/

company focusing on a customer-driven feedback loop and have a solid developer or team of developers on-site, then a small batch process such as Agile is the right choice.

The following lists provide a quick comparison of Agile and Waterfall pros and cons.

AGILE CONSIDERATIONS	WATERFALL CONSIDERATIONS
Creative and discovery-driven projects	Transactional projects (black-and-white requirements)
Seeks product-market fit	Precise control of time and cost
Team typically on-site together	Mission-critical system development
Responsive to changing requirements	Clients with external vendors
Responsive user-feedback loop	Remote teams work well
Small teams (five to nine) of mostly senior developers	Large teams (20 or more)
Quick initial product release	Teams with junior engineers
Intensity of iterations can lead to burnout	Better documentation

Takeaways

- Lean methodology provides a conceptual framework for discovering product-market fit, by involving customers early and often in the design process.

- Use wireframes to quickly iterate user-experience prototypes with your customer prospects. This will provide tremendous time savings compared to building a functional product for review.

- Agile methodology is an efficient method for iterative development. It's a good complement to Lean methodology, particularly for early-stage product development. However, it's not right for every project or team.

- Don't worry about building a perfect system in the early stages; focus on rapid prototyping instead. Frequent pivots and changes will invalidate most early assumptions.

CHAPTER 9

GOING TO MARKET

> "In the modern world of business, it is useless to be a creative, original thinker unless you can also sell what you create."
>
> —DAVID OGILVY

After your product has been built and you've discovered and adapted to find market fit, the next step is to begin to market your business. Many startups focus entirely on their product or service offering and fail to acknowledge how important marketing and advertising are. Still others waste considerable money on inappropriate marketing channels before discovering what really works for their product. There are a few observable patterns you can apply to get to your goals a bit faster.

In this chapter, we'll review the primary online marketing channels and explore which of these might work best for each of the eight models identified in Chapter 6, "Business Models."

Internet marketing channels

At the turn of the century, Internet marketing was simple. You could either add a few keywords to your website to get more exposure from the popular search engines of the time (AltaVista and Yahoo!) or send email offers en masse to every email address you could harvest while scraping the web. Over time these channels have evolved better regulations and new channels been introduced. Today there are seven distinct marketing channels online. Some of these will apply to your particular business more than others, but it's worthwhile going through each one for context.

Organic search (SEO)

Many people start their online session by searching Google, Bing, or Yahoo! for what they need. As such, the search engines are well positioned to send significant relevant traffic to sites that rank for popular terms in these results. The standard unpaid listings of the search result pages are called organic search results, and the method of ranking well in these organic listings is known as search engine optimization (SEO).

There are three primary elements of a successful SEO campaign: accessibility, content, and citations. Accessibility is a matter of user-interface architure. Is your site structured such that users and crawlers can quickly access your content, or is it somehow obscured either by the structure, navigation, or embedded technologies you are using? The page also needs to be properly tagged to help search engines to understand the significance of important key phrases. Assuming the pages are easily accessed, content is the next element that matters. Having plentiful well-written content that contains keywords you want to rank for is like the seed that you are planting. But like any seed, water is needed in order for anything to happen. Inbound links from credible external websites are the metaphoric water than helps your content to grow. These citations are what validates the quality of your content and signals its importance to relevancy search engines.

Paid search (PPC)

The highlighted search results on the top and right of a search engine results page are typically paid placement advertisements. Google AdWords is the name of Google's program through which you would purchase these; Bing Ads is where you would purchase paid placement advertisements for both Bing and Yahoo! Google has also developed a rather extensive ad placement network that allows you to place text, banner, and video ads throughout its network, which spans YouTube and the AdSense network, including millions of blogs and mobile applications. By paying per click (PPC), you can have your advertisement placed in these ad positions and drive additional traffic to your site, regardless of your organic search rankings.

Ad banners (retargeting)

These are the original form of online advertisement. An advertiser can place ad units on popular websites around the web to help drive brand awareness. Ad banners are typically priced on a CPM basis (cost per 1,000 impressions) rather than per click in the case of PPC ads. Because ad banners are best for brand awareness, most direct-marketing type businesses do not find the return on ad spend to be worthwhile. However, retargeting has substantially increased the value of ad banners for all types of advertisers. By participating in large ad distribution networks such as Google's DoubleClick and AdSense, it's possible to track users' movements on the web and target specific ads to them based on where they've been previously. The most popular form of retargeting is trailing a user after he's visited your website to continue to show ads for your brand and reinforce that initial interest. This ensures that a potential prospect will receive numerous exposures to your brand over a period of time after visiting your site.

Social (presence, outreach)

Social is a term that refers to properties such as Facebook, Twitter, LinkedIn, Google+, and StumbleUpon. These properties serve two functions: maintaining a brand presence where consumers may want to interact with you, and reaching prospective customers or clients.

Facebook, Google+, and StumbleUpon can help make your brand more prominent. By publishing content regularly to your feed and holding contests, you can stay top of mind with your audience and keep them engaged. Google+ is also part of the Google organic search results feedback loop and can further augment brand presence for that reason. Social sites can also be useful for outreach at more of a business-to-business level. Publishing to your Twitter or LinkedIn feeds, participating in online conversations, and joining groups can help you establish relationships with new clients.

Email (drip and alerts)

Email can add significant back-end value to other channels by enabling semi-automated sales lead incubation. If a sales conversion fails or is delayed due to the size of the purchase, email can keep these leads engaged and possibly bring them back to complete the sale, thus augmenting the total ROI of the front-facing advertising vehicle that generated the lead. In the case of SaaS and ecommerce models, alert emails can be sent as key opportunities arise to reengage the lead, such as a sale event or an event in the user's free trial SaaS account. Drip emails can be set up as an automated sequence to follow up with the lead on scheduled intervals to drive value and further prime the lead to take action.

Product feeds

Ecommerce sites can bring greater exposure and compete against larger brands on a price basis by having products listed in comparison shopping engines (CSEs) such as Google Product Search, NexTag, Amazon Marketplace, and Shopzilla. These CSEs uptake XML data feeds that describe a merchant's products, aggregate this data, and display competing products and prices from participating merchants when a consumer searches for a product. The merchant is charged per click for every sales lead driven back to the merchant's website. Thus product feeds provide an incremental opportunity for ecommerce businesses to reach new customers and qualified leads.

Affiliate marketing

Many SaaS companies and product vendors have found success by augmenting their marketing efforts with independent resellers (affiliates) who perform online marketing on behalf of the brand. Affiliates are typically compensated with revenue share (percentage commission) and generate money by acquiring traffic for less than their share of the revenue. Affiliates tend to be more aggressive with their tactics than a brand would be since they have no accountability if the brand is damaged. Thus it's important to set limits on acceptable traffic and marketing conduct. Nevertheless, many brands find harmony with affiliates that play in the gray areas at an arm's length and add incrementally to sales.

Marketing funnel stages

In 1898, E. St. Elmo Lewis defined the stages of engagement within an advertisement. The specific application was to the structure of marketing copy in an ad, but his observation can be applied to the macro-level relationship between a marketer and a prospect as well, that is, the stages of engagement from the first advertising touchpoint to a purchase event that may not occur until months later.

The attention stage describes new business prospecting in the purest sense. You're seeking new clients or customers and simply trying to let them know your offering is in the market. Once you have their attention, you can begin to build their interest with your value proposition, making a case for why your offering is better than that of your competitors. In the desire stage, you may begin to leverage the prospects' interest into action with offers and direct sales tactics. Finally, in the action stage, you shepherd the prospect through the process of the purchase transaction. This model for classifying the stages of conversion is known as AIDA (attention, interest, desire, action: **Figure 9.1**).

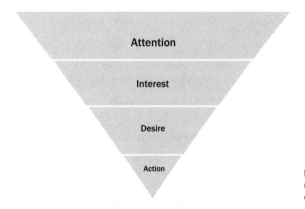

Figure 9.1 AIDA (attention, interest, desire, action).

Consider how this might be relevant to your own marketing activities. If you're marketing a higher-price product or service, your prospect will spend more time researching and qualifying your offering. For this reason you might focus your time on the higher-funnel stages of action and interest, providing research information and consultation, a type of marketing known as inbound marketing. Conversely, if you're marketing a lower-risk and better-known commodity product, there's little value to nursing higher-funnel introductions. In this case, there's a good chance your prospect already knows that he needs to purchase your offering, so you'd be better off focusing on harvesting those prospects in the desire and action stages—an approach more aligned with outbound techniques.

This delineation affects your messaging and marketing channels as well. Direct marketing techniques such as scarcity, price competition, or incentive offers might work well for trying to close a quantitative sale (for example, a commodity product), but would fall flat for qualitative purchase decisions. You're much more likely to engage that prospect by speaking to his needs at that stage of the process, providing research and answering questions.

Some marketing channels are implicitly higher in the sales funnel than others. For example, social rarely converts directly to a sale but it can influence later sales if you connect with the prospect and offer support now. Give away knowledge in the form of whitepapers or free analysis and check in periodically to offer help and advice, so the prospect will come to you when he's ready. Paid search conversely is well aligned with direct marketing techniques and is well positioned at the bottom of the sales funnel. Use it to capitalize on a prospect who's actively searching for a purchase opportunity in some cases. This is the rationale behind focusing on longer phrases for paid search that indicate a readiness to buy, rather than generic terms that may signal the user is not about to buy.

Internet marketing models

There are three different marketing models that can be generically applied to every business model: placement, inbound, and outbound (**Figure 9.2**). Every business should make placement its first order of business, but on top of that foundation every business is inherently either inbound or outbound in focus. Inbound businesses concentrate more on building their reputation and indirectly building referrals, while outbound businesses focus more on direct sales and marketing efforts that drive near-term profits.

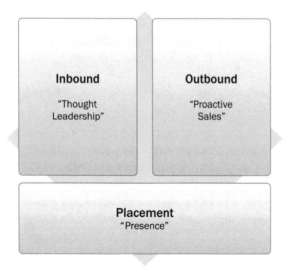

Figure 9.2
Marketing stack.

Placement

The first step of marketing any new business online is placement (**Figure 9.3**). Regardless of whether your primary long-term efforts focus on inbound or outbound marketing, prospective clients and customers will look up your business and try to learn more about you. Organic search rankings are also affected by a lack of placement. So you need to establish a professional presence, be easy to find, and control your brand message before you begin promoting yourself.

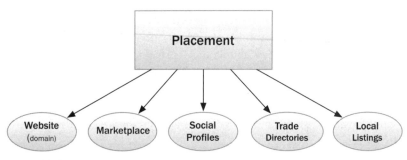

Figure 9.3 Placement.

To accomplish this goal, secure any related domain names or user names on popular social sites and occupy them. If you have a graphic brand identity, make sure this is consistently expressed across the web. You may also want to consider registering your brand as a trademark with the U.S. Patent and Trademark Office at the same time.[1]

Make sure your brand is listed on important trade directories. For example, you would want to list an SaaS tax product on AccountantsWorld, an SEO consulting service on TopSEOs.com. For an ecommerce business, you might want to establish product feeds for placement in comparison search engines as well. If you're selling a product, make sure it's available in the relevant marketplaces. If you're a retailer, you need to have your product feeds placed with Amazon, Google Product Search, and Shopzilla. And if you have a local office, make sure it's listed with popular local search tools like Google Maps, Yellowpages.com, and Yelp.

---

1 http://uspto.gov

Once you've taken steps to establish your brand's foundation online, you're ready to begin with proactive marketing efforts, either with an inbound or an outbound marketing plan.

Inbound marketing

Inbound marketing is about selling indirectly through thought leadership. The focus is on education, publishing research, or otherwise conveying an understanding of a given topic. Your goal is to brand yourself as an expert and ensure that those who are researching can find you. The idea is that by focusing your efforts on pursuing excellence, you will naturally establish a superior brand position from which you can charge higher prices or rates and attract the best clients and customers.

Inbound marketing is generally appropriate for more sophisticated purchase decisions in which the client or customer is doing research to identify a suitable product or service (**Figure 9.4**). Your goal is to capture his attention and position yourself as the best option by allowing the consumer to come to his own conclusions during his research. Thus you're focusing on higher-funnel marketing channels that speak most directly to the attention and interest stages (AIDA).

Figure 9.4
Inbound marketing.

Organic search, ad banners, and social sites can be great ways to introduce your brand to these prospects and to get them into your lead-nurturing campaign. A lead-nurturing campaign is heavily focused on the development of great content and on distributing that content via email, social sites, and your company blog. You may even consider being present at key events and tradeshows as well as speaking appearances and other opportunities to reach out to prospects to advise them on solving their problems.

Inbound marketing is also sometimes called content marketing for its focus on creating great content. This content takes the form of a blog, video, infographics, or just about anything consumable and shareable. Sometimes you may post this content to your own blog, though other times you might post it as a guest blog post on prominent blog sites in your community in order to seed better exposure and drive traffic (and link citations) back to your primary website. And there's always an eye on how to make your content more "viral" in order to have social sites carry your message to more recipients than you could possibly reach directly. Thus humorous infographics and videos are popular.

The two primary drivers of traffic to an inbound marketing brand's website are typically organic search rankings and social sites. So aside from the primary activity of generating great content, the secondary activity is seeking external citations for that content in the form of inbound links from other websites and social mentions ("likes" and "shares"). The inbound links have a direct impact on search rankings in the major search engines. Social mentions have a direct impact on the amount of visibility that content will receive on those social sites, but it also has an indirect impact on search results now that search engines like Google are considering social mentions as part of a quality signal.[2]

Inbound marketing brands and professionals frequently seek opportunities to extend their brand beyond the online world by participating in speaking engagements and industry conferences, teaching courses at the local college, and positioning themselves to be interviewed for major publications and news organizations.

---

2 http://www.seomoz.org/blog/the-impact-of-authoritative-links-mentions-and-shares-on-rankings

Outbound marketing

Outbound marketing is more about direct marketing than branding, and focuses on the lower-funnel stages of desire and action (AIDA). Inbound marketing is driven by long-term reputation and establishing a higher branding position, while outbound marketing focuses more on near-term return on ad spend (ROAS). As great as the hyperbole may sound with inbound marketing, the reality is that outbound marketing is simply more effective for some types of businesses (**Figure 9.5**).

Figure 9.5
Outbound marketing.

Efforts typically focus on paid search rather than organic results. While paid search can be expensive, it's also highly measurable, controllable, and predictable. A business can thus measure how any paid search campaign is performing and optimize those campaigns down to the nickel to ensure profitability.

Organic search can still be a part of the search strategy for an outbound company, though the approach is driven by revenue—rather than quality signals—and thus is approached differently. Frequently these efforts are inclined toward "gray hat" techniques that can help to expedite returns. Affiliate marketing can be another channel to effectively increment sales with little capital risk, since affiliate partners are paid on a revenue-share basis.

The business focused on direct sales is rarely interested in investing deeply into a meaningful content marketing campaign, which would drive the higher-funnel branding efforts and better organic search rankings, particularly since the return on those efforts is not measurable. This is perfectly reasonable for a certain type of company. If you're selling commodity products online, for example, the prospect is likely already convinced of the need for the product, he's merely looking to purchase from the most convenient or lowest-price vendor. And for this reason, the value of consultative selling is mitigated; the reseller of commodity products rightfully should focus on lower-funnel conversions, not brand building or facilitation of research.

Outbound marketers are typically quite aware and proactive about managing their sales funnel. Employing back-end assist techniques such as "warm" telemarketing and using email drip/auto-responder campaigns can help to incubate or even reengage sales leads originally acquired through front-end marketing channels such as PPC, affiliates, and search traffic generation methods, and further increase returns on ad spend.

Choosing a marketing model

When considering inbound versus outbound marketing techniques, essentially what you are deciding is whether to focus your marketing efforts lower in the funnel, closer to the transaction, or higher in the funnel, where new introductions are made and longer-term brand building occurs (**Figure 9.6**). To determine which of these approaches would be best for your business, ask yourself whether you have the potential to influence an audience and retain longer-term relationships with them, or are you competing primarily on price or the ability to sell?

Alas, nothing is ever entirely black and white. While the resell of airline tickets is highly skewed toward outbound marketing and consulting services skewed toward inbound marketing, there are many other businesses that fall somewhere in between, and that would benefit from both types of marketing. A wine reseller, for example, might drive traffic for standard types of purchases such as gift baskets or popular bottles of wine via standard outbound marketing channels. That same wine reseller, however, could also benefit from inbound marketing efforts, by showcasing their knowledge of wine and demonstrating their large inventory of harder-to-find or premium wines. This would help them to capture the longer-tail audience, who very well might be more loyal patrons over time.

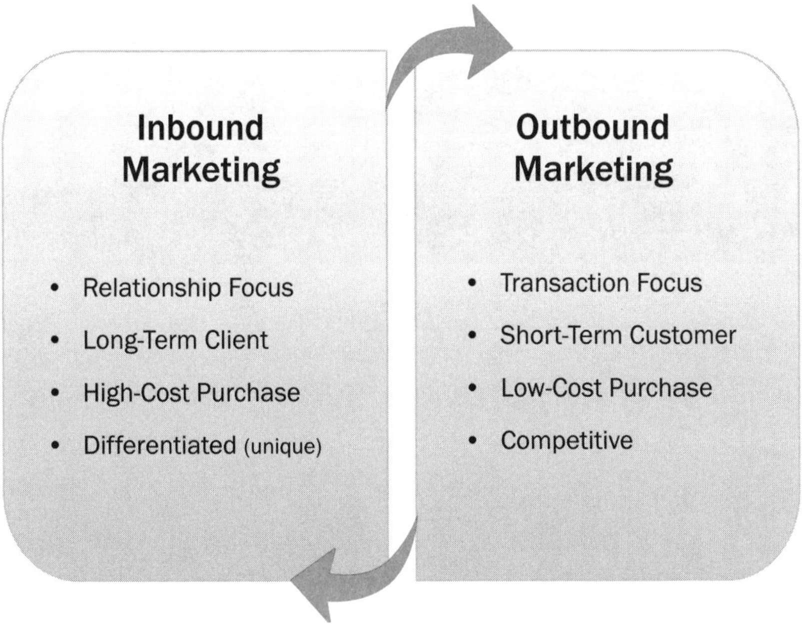

Inbound Marketing	Outbound Marketing
• Relationship Focus	• Transaction Focus
• Long-Term Client	• Short-Term Customer
• High-Cost Purchase	• Low-Cost Purchase
• Differentiated (unique)	• Competitive

Figure 9.6 Marketing models.

Other types of businesses can be segmented based on the market they are selling into. Software as a product or software as a service, for example, might be sold with outbound marketing techniques in mature markets where the domain is well understood and competition is fierce. In newer markets where the value of the software is not as well known, however, inbound marketing may be more effective. In such an environment you could build a brand upon the moral authority of being first to market and thus focus on selling the value of your solution and the insights of your company, rather than competing for sales and transactions.

Takeaways

- Placement is the first step to establishing an online presence. Ensure your business is easily found in the search engines and professional directories where your prospects are searching.

- Inbound marketing focuses on establishing a reputation within the community. It appeals to prospects, who are seeking to qualify a business for expensive purchases or long-term professional relationships.

- Outbound marketing focuses on converting qualified leads that are ready to convert. This approach is appropriate for commodity purchases, that are sensitive to price or convenience, rather than reputation.

CHAPTER 10

OPTIMIZATION

"Most people use statistics the way a
drunkard uses a lamp post, more for
support than illumination."

—MARK TWAIN

The Internet is an increasingly crowded and competitive place. In economic terms, the Internet is an efficient marketplace, in which the cost of acquiring traffic has quickly risen to level at or just below what the average vendor can monetize that traffic for. This is especially true in auction-based ad markets such as Google AdWords, but the effects of increased competition are evident everywhere. Search engine optimization (SEO) was once seen as a bastion of free traffic for those who couldn't afford direct marketing channels such as pay per click (PPC). Companies could apply a little effort and get considerable traffic without much cost. But today the increasing complexity and competition of ranking organically makes the indirect cost inevitable.

All of this has the potential to leave new startups in an unfortunate position. You may have a viable offering for your market but simply can't afford to drive much traffic; you've been relegated to the relatively insignificant amount of traffic you can afford based on the earnings you're getting off that traffic. Fortunately there is a solution: optimization.

You need to turn your attention back to your online presence to determine how you can get more sales for every dollar spent acquiring new customers. If you can increase your return on ad spend (ROAS), you can afford higher ad costs. And once you can afford those, you can suddenly drive a lot more traffic to your site and the virtuous cycle begins.

After you've started to acquire traffic, there are three activities you can focus on to maximize the value of that traffic. The first is traffic optimization, in which you start looking more critically at the quality of traffic you're receiving and what you're paying for it. The second is conversion optimization, in which you're looking to convert those visitors into a first sale with your brand. The third is customer retention, which focuses on extracting additional value from existing customers who have already purchased from you. Traffic optimization, conversion optimization, and customer retention have an amplification effect on one another when looking at the ROAS (**Figure 10.1**).

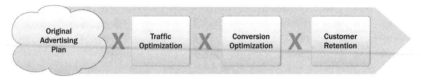

Figure 10.1 The amplification effect of optimization.

To illustrate this point, let's assume that you're going to spend $100 on PPC ads to acquire two customers ($1 per click; $50 customer acquisition cost). Each new customer makes a purchase of $50, and there's a $20 unit cost, which gives you a $30 net profit per customer, before advertising costs. Two units sold give you $60 in profits. Unfortunately we spent $100 on advertising, so we're actually net negative by $40 (ROI minus 28 percent). This illustrates what many startups first experience with paid search: they can't make money with it. Fortunately, there are a few things you can do.

First, let's look at traffic optimization. By paying attention to keywords that are profitable and testing variations of the ad copy, you can not only improve your base conversion rate, but also improve the quality score assigned to your ad, which means you'll be paying much less per click.

If you're successful in lowering the quality score enough to drive twice as much traffic with the same ad budget, and conservatively assuming all other variables such as conversion rate stay the same to keep things simple, you've already doubled your effectiveness and pulled yourself up to a positive ROI with this one effort alone (ROI of 11 percent).

Next let's look inside the site for opportunities to improve the conversion rate of visitors to the site. With the help of analytics metrics and testing tools, you find and correct usability issues and improve marketing copy to appeal more to your users. In the process, you increase the conversion rate by 25 percent, a number that is entirely realistic for a new product that has not yet been optimized. Through this effort you raise gross revenue by another $50 and bring the total ROI to 25 percent.

Finally, let's look at customer retention, which has a further compounding effect. By paying attention to your customer outreach and loyalty programs, you can extend your relationship with existing customers, rather than spending money to acquire new ones.

Let's assume you're able to generate an average of one more sale per customer. You'll have unit costs ($20), of course, but no additional acquisition cost, so the value of subsequent sales is significantly higher than another new sale from a newly acquired customer. As a result of this and building on the compounded optimization you've done with acquisition and conversion, you double your sales in this step, but *quadruple* your net profits, for a final ROI of 67 percent on the original $100 spend.

For many startups, increasing the returns on ad spend this much can be game changing. It can mean finally being able to profitably and reliably acquire traffic. It also means being able to afford higher-cost media channels, which can give you access to substantially more customers; you can turn on the fire hose, so to speak. Once you're able to do that, you can begin to scale your business rapidly.

And so we begin our last chapter, a discussion of optimization. We'll cover effective use of behavioral analytics to provide actionable insights, a systematic approach to testing for conversion optimization, and attention to retaining existing customers to get more out of each customer. Collectively these activities can significantly impact your bottom line, enabling you to compete in the competitive online ecosystem.

Table 10.1 Optimization calculations

	ORIGINAL	TRAFFIC (+100%)	CONVERSION (+25%)	RETENTION (+100%)
Traffic quantity	100	200	200	200
CPC	$1.00	$0.50	$0.50	$0.50
Conversion rate	2%	2%	2.50%	N/A
Advertising cost	$100	$100	$100	$100
Units sold	2	4	5	10
Unit price	$50	$50	$50	$50
Unit cost	$20	$20	$20	$20
Gross revenue (sold * price)	$100	$200	$250	$500
Total cost (units + ads)	($140)	($180)	($200)	($300)
Net profit	($40)	$20	$50	$200
ROAS (revenue/ad spend)	100%	200%	250%	500%
ROI ([revenue-costs]/costs)	-28%	11%	25%	67%

Analytics-driven insights

It's remarkable to see what actionable insights you can derive from web analytics with proper instrumentation. Too few entrepreneurs make full use of the tools, however. A common scenario is to install Google Analytics and check in each week to see how much traffic is coming to your web application. This passive approach yields relatively little actionable data you can use to either improve ROAS or user engagement.

The solution is a proactive, key performance indicators (KPI)-driven approach to analytics. Start by defining success criteria and look at how you can instrument your site so that analytics give you information that directly speaks to your stated goals. These will be your KPI. For example, a goal might be to achieve a sales conversion, have a user fill out a lead-generation form, or view a certain number of pages of content and stay on the site for a stated amount of time. If you can state a goal, there's probably a way to track it.

There are several effective behavioral analytics applications available, but considering we are talking about startups, we are going to assume the use of Google Analytics for the balance of this discussion. Google Analytics (GA) provides excellent tracking and reporting tools for no cost, and can go a long way toward accomplishing our insight and optimization goals. We will also discuss a couple other useful tools along the way, which augment our tools and insights.

Conversion tracking

Arguably the most important aspect of analytics is the ability to track the achievement of goals per user session. Let's assume a key performance indicator for your business is to get users to purchase an item from your online store. Google Analytics provides a tracking code that you can embed on your receipt page that helps it register a success event for a given user session. Once you've defined a goal, you can also specify a sequence of pages or events that should occur leading up to the conversion event. This page sequence is called your conversion funnel.

Using conversion funnels, you're able to track where users fall off along the funnel sequence prior to completing a goal (**Figure 10.2**). This can be immensely helpful for diagnosing bottlenecks in your funnel sequence, and resolving those issues can help lift your overall conversion rate.

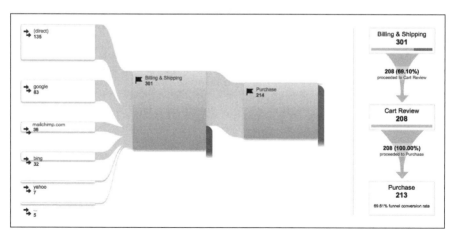

Figure 10.2 Google Analytics conversion funnel visualization.

Let's suppose that your overall conversion rate is less than industry averages, so you begin to look for abnormal falloff in your funnel sequence. You observe a significant drop-off from checkout to your confirmation page. This is a signal to look more closely at your checkout page for a problem. Look for apparent usability issues such as instructions that are unclear, a Submit button that's hidden below the fold, or an error in the form validation that's keeping some of your users from completing checkout.

Once you know where to look for a problem, the answer may become obvious. If not, this may simply be an opportunity for A/B testing, a technique we'll discuss later, as part of conversion optimization.

Traffic segmentation

Visitor segmentation is another helpful resource that enables you to look at data for certain cross sections of your population. For example, you could segment your data to look only at users from California, then compare your funnel and conversion activity to Oregon to get a sense of how local weather or culture might be affecting conversions. You could segment across a number of different dimensions, and spend time exploring these dimensions to identify patterns that could be meaningful for ad budget optimization purposes.

Let's assume you have a mobile version of your website. What if you determine that 10 percent of your visitors are using mobile but few of them convert? You may even find as you dig more deeply that the majority of your mobile purchases are coming from iPads, with very few from iPhones or Android devices. That could be useful information for improving your website with better responsive design for iPhones or Android devices, or simply limiting your paid advertisements.

Multi-touch attribution

If you've already set up funnels and goals to track key performance indicators, then congratulations on taking that step. But there's more to this story. Conversions are often not a straight line, so a linear funnel can sometimes be an oversimplification of the actual sale process of more complex and higher-priced purchases (**Figure 10.3**).

Figure 10.3 A more complex conversion funnel.

Take the decision to buy a nice watch. A shopper may spend several days or weeks researching and comparison-shopping before actually purchasing the item. It's entirely possible that the prospect may visit your site once or twice on separate occasions before deciding to purchase. Let's say the first visit came from organic search and the second came from a paid ad banner. On that second visit, the user signs up for a newsletter. A few days later he was sent a coupon for 10 percent off all watches and, based on receiving that offer, the prospect completed the order online. To which of these channels do you credit the sale?

In the absence of multi-touch attribution reporting, most analytics tools are "last touch"-centric, meaning they would give credit to the last touch before the sales transaction—in this case, the newsletter. But that's a shortsighted perspective considering you probably paid for an ad campaign that sent the customer to the site in the first place, where she signed up for the newsletter. And perhaps she was open to clicking the ad banner because she'd already been to the website a couple days prior, via organic search results. Clearly, all of these events played some role in nurturing the sale (**Figure 10.4**). In multi-touch attribution, we call those prior touchpoints "assists."

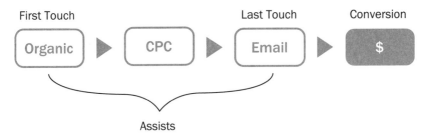

Figure 10.4 Multi-touch attribution exposes assisting referrals.

This is an important concept when considering ad budget allocation. Some advertising channels (and certain keywords) are lower in the conversion funnel and more likely to convert on that same visit. Pay-per-click advertising, for example, converts very effectively for long-tail key phrases, particularly for lower-price commodity products.

Social media on the other hand is very high in the funnel. As such, it may make brand introductions or help to nurture a lead that will pay off later, but not necessarily while a purchase is imminent. For this reason, it may seem to convert poorly when only attributing to the last click. But if you look more deeply at the assists over the course of that conversion life cycle, you're likely to find that there's more credit due to upper-funnel channels than you first thought.

As you look back on all the activity of a funnel, you may be wondering how to properly value each of those touchpoints. Attribution modeling is a complex topic and each business should consider it carefully as it pertains to its own business (**Figure 10.5**). We generally recommend starting with a time-decay model, which gives decreasing credit attributed to each touchpoint the further back in time you go. Another popular model is the horseshoe model, which gives equal weight to the first and last touchpoints and less credit to any touches in the middle.

When you consider all of this, you'll quickly see this is an opportunity to optimize your ad budget. In the absence of multi-touch attribution, you might give too much credit to low-funnel activities and too little credit to higher-funnel activities. Think about how this presents an opportunity to optimize your ROAS.

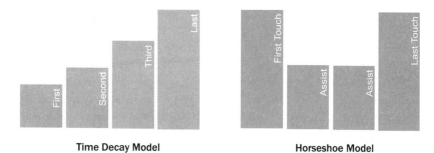

Time Decay Model   Horseshoe Model

Figure 10.5 Examples of attribution modeling.

These are just a few examples of the resources available in behavioral analytics tools such as Google Analytics to gain actionable insights into user behavior. You can use this knowledge to drive ad budget optimization or to pinpoint issues in page flow that may signal usability issues that need to be addressed.

Traffic optimization

Traffic optimization is the first step in the amplification model. The goal is simple: increase your ROAS by improving the effectiveness of your advertising and channel engagement. Whether talking about spending money on paid search, investing in organic search rankings, or building a social presence, the fundamental goal is the same.

In an increasingly noisy online marketing world, you must have a highly focused message and concentrate your efforts around that message in order to reach your customers. This will give you more potent organic listings that are more easily achieved, paid search campaigns with superior returns, and social newsfeed content that's more likely to be shared and published.

Semantics

Building on the customer persona and user story you developed in
Chapter 3, "Do Your Research," let's begin to focus our marketing message to match your target market. Popular tools such as Wordtracker.com
and KeywordDiscovery.com provide a database you can query to determine key phrases and search volume for those phrases, related to primary
terms in a market segment. This can be invaluable for discovering long-
tail phrases that, because of their specificity, may indicate nuance about
your customers' needs. It may also suggest interests you can focus on to
become more relevant to that segment. That's the kind of insight that can
drive effective messaging that drives conversions.

This knowledge isn't just important for planning your marketing efforts.
Specific long-phrase terms also have tactical significance by indicating
that a prospect is close to a purchase decision, meaning these terms
can provide high conversions compared to related generic terms. For
example, consider the difference between someone searching for "Toyota
Camry" versus "2013 Toyota Camry Los Angeles." The first search query
could be a casual, high-funnel prospect who won't convert anytime soon,
or someone looking for an owner's manual for a car she already owns.
The second query would likely send you the higher-quality lead.

If your goal is ranking in organic search results, these more specific key
phrases will be much less competitive and thus easier to rank for. That
means arranging fewer inbound links and writing less SEO content, thus
a lower cost to rank. You'll get considerably less traffic for each of these
terms, of course, but you just might find that these terms are still deliver-
ing a good number of converting visitors, despite less volume. This has a
considerable impact on ROI.

The same is true in paid search. Competition for long-tail phrases will be
considerably lower, so your cost per click (CPC) will typically be less. If
the term is a close-to-purchase actionable phrase, you'll likely find that
your revenue is also higher, despite the lower acquisition costs.

A more focused message will also perform better with social networks.
With all the noise in everyone's newsfeed, the odds of getting someone to
share something are low. You're more likely to accomplish this goal if you
have a highly targeted message that resonates with a few, rather than trying to post something moderately interesting to everyone.

Algorithms

Most online marketing channels are subject to some form of automated filtering or prioritization algorithm that can impact the performance of your campaign. Whether we're talking about organic search, paid search, social sites, or video channels, the challenge and the solution are fundamentally the same at a high level. You need a tightly focused message and marketing campaign that is small enough to be highly effective and relevant. If it's too diffuse, the odds of getting lost in the noise of your competition is high. Let's illustrate this point with a few examples:

ORGANIC SEARCH

Search engines base much of their search rankings on quality, relevant content, and supporting inbound links that affirm the significance of the website. Because there's so much great content online today, a search engine may have a large number of quality articles that deserve a high ranking for a search query. To help prioritize these articles, the search engine will look at how many links each source has, and the quality of those links.[1] The solution is to focus on a specific market segment that you can afford to compete in. The more focused your message, the more likely it is that you'll succeed in developing a competitive base of content and the supporting backlink profile.

PAID SEARCH

Both Google AdWords and Bing Ads use an ad scoring algorithm that can have a significant impact on the amount you pay per click for your advertisement. The score is determined by looking at how relevant the content of the ad is, compared to the key phrase you've bid for and the content of the landing page. The key to achieving a high-quality score is managing smaller ad groups with no more than 10 to 12 key phrases per group. Ideally, you would also have a separate landing page for each ad group that reflects this tightly focused key phrase cluster on the landing page itself, to reaffirm relevance.[2] By taking this approach, your ads will naturally have higher relevance and thus, a higher-quality score and a lower cost per click.

---

1 http://en.wikipedia.org/wiki/Backlink

2 http://support.google.com/adwords/bin/answer.py?hl=en&answer=2454010

SOCIAL NETWORKS (FACEBOOK)

Even the social networks have introduced content-filtering algorithms to help separate signal from noise (spam), on behalf of their users. Facebook in particular has an algorithm called EdgeRank that looks at criteria such as user affinity toward the source, weight of the content type and source, and time decay to determine whether to publish a story for a given user. Think long term about how to build your affinity rank with your users by publishing highly relevant posts that receive ample shares and likes.

Conversion optimization

Conversion optimization is the practice of improving user experience and testing marketing copy and design to increase the percentage of visitors who complete a desired event. That event could be a purchase, completion of a lead-generation form, or signup for a trial account.

Effective conversion optimization starts with considering effective user experience and addressing any issues that may be causing confusion, frustration, or concern. Once those issues have been addressed, the effort becomes more about creating effective marketing copy, images, and value propositions that resonate with your prospect.

Taking the time to address these issues can result in double- or even triple-digit improvements in conversion rates for some types of sites. Considering that the value of such conversion increases would meet or exceed the profit margins many companies work within for sales, this is a clear opportunity to improve your ability to acquire traffic profitably.

Experimentation

If no obvious usability issues are discovered while using analytics to study the page flow of your funnels (as discussed above), the next step is to begin experimentation. For many of the larger Internet brands, testing is a long-term and ongoing commitment. They are constantly studying their target demographic and developing new concepts they believe will provide additional lift.

As an example of the extent some companies go to with testing, Marissa Mayer famously asked her team at Google to test 41 shades of blue buttons to determine which shade would yield a higher click rate.[3] As a startup you may not benefit sufficiently from such attention to detail to necessitate it. It does, however, illustrate the value of testing and how seriously some companies take it—and why you should too!

Two forms of experimentation are common in conversion optimization: split (A/B) and multivariate testing. Split testing is the most common as well as the most appropriate for smaller sites with relatively less traffic (**Figure 10.6**). It allows you to test different versions of a page to determine which version will outperform the other.

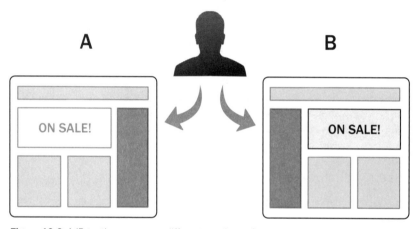

Figure 10.6 A/B testing compares different versions of a page.

Multivariate testing on the other hand, enables concurrent testing of discreet elements that may span multiple pages. Its primary advantage is testing of interaction effects that result from compounding different elements. Multivariate testing requires signficiant traffic volume, however, and much of the low-lying fruit is more easily captured by smaller businesses and startups by focusing on split (A/B) testing.

---

3 http://www.fastcompany.com/1403230/googles-marissa-mayer-assaults-designers-data

Google Analytics includes a tool called Content Experiments (formerly Google Website Optimizer), which is a great way to run your tests. Other tools such as Visual Website Optimizer, Optimizely, and Unbounce provide more robust paid alternatives as well. All of these tools share the same fundamental premise: you can run numerous versions of a page to determine which one will lead to a conversion more frequently. After enough traffic is gathered, your testing tool will tell you within a specified degree of confidence which test scenario is going to be your best performer.

Getting in the mindset

As you begin designing your test scenarios, you'll likely wonder about best practices you can build around. For example, you may have heard about B.O.B., the Big Orange Button that converts better than any other type of button. Or that you should remove your navigation bar on sign-up pages to keep the user focused on the action you want her to take. While there may be a handful of usability tips to be found, the reality is that every audience is different, every context is different, and you need to run your own experiments to know what will resonate with your customers. There are, however, a few guiding principles that can help you design more effective test cases:

USER EXPERIENCE

As you look at your page-flow sequence, consider what makes a good user experience. Is the interface intuitive and easy to understand? Have you reinforced a sense of trust? Is there congruity between your brand position and what you're asking of the user? Think about how these principles might drive the design of your navigation, page layout, and forms. If a prospect can't locate a "Submit" button because it's below the fold of the browser window, that's a real usability problem. Equally, a form that's too long and requests too much personal information may invoke trust issues. Think about how you can address these issues and remove roadblocks that might keep the user from completing the desired action.

USER-CENTERED DESIGN

It's important to deeply understand your target demographic. This understanding will drive the composition of your marketing copy, your calls to action, and your selection of supporting images. Try creating a persona (as discussed in Chapter 3) that defines the key attributes of a person you can market to. Give your persona a name and determine his or her age, occupation, marital status, hobbies, and so on. Also consider the persona's user story. What role is she playing when visiting your site and what is her task? Perhaps she's an employee tasked with researching a purchase for an executive. Or she may be making a decision for herself. This difference could significantly impact how you want to engage this prospect. Understanding your customers and their motivations is the first step to connecting with them more deeply by speaking more effectively to their needs.

EXPECTATIONS

Don't expect to see improvements with every test scenario you design. By its very nature, experimentation is a process of discovering what works. It's well known that what may work for one group doesn't necessarily work for another. In fact, optimization professionals are often surprised to see the outcomes of their experiments, even after years of practice. Anne Holland's website WhichTestWon.com demonstrates this point. On the site, optimization professionals are asked to share their testing scenarios for the community to guess which scenarios were more effective. It illustrates how even experts in the field can't consistently predict the outcome of a test. So take a cue from this example and make testing an ongoing part of your process.

Customer retention

What are you doing to retain your customers after the first purchase? According to the book *Customer Winback* by Jill Griffin and Michael Lowenstein, sales campaigns marketed toward existing customers can have success rates as high as 70 percent.[4] This number may not apply to every market vertical or business model, but it does illustrate a point. Consider the cost of acquiring new customers and what that does to your net profit per sale. Now imagine if you could get your average customer to buy twice instead of just once and consider that impact on the net profits from each customer you acquire. You'll quickly see the benefit of retaining and nurturing the customers you already have.

---

4 Jill Griffin and Michael W. Lowenstein (2001), *Customer Winback: How to Recapture Lost Customers... And Keep Them Loyal* Jossey-Bass

Customer service

How well are you taking care of your customers? According to a Bain & Company study, 80 percent of companies interviewed indicated that they had superior customer service.[5] Yet only 8 percent of customers interviewed on their experiences with those companies agreed. That's a sobering statistic that should leave every company thinking about why and what they should be doing differently.

Despite good intentions, it seems that part of the problem may be a misalignment of priorities. According to the research firm CRM Guru, most companies, particularly small firms, focus principally on features and price.[6] But customers rated customer service three to five times more important than either features or price in determining whether they would stay loyal to that business.

Clearly, customer service is important to customers and it's easy to understand why. We've all had the experience of a product or service not working properly. If we can't resolve our challenges with a product or service, then the solution is of little value or no value, and it no longer justifies the cost. Now consider how many online companies provide no phone number or any other way to contact customer service for real-time support. Even the option to submit a ticket is sometimes buried and accessible only after checking to ensure that an answer to a question isn't already in the company's self-help knowledge base.

If this sounds like your customer support approach, it may be time to take a step back and reevaluate your customers' interaction with your business. Consider this a user-experience issue and approach it as you would with optimizing your conversion funnel; look for bottlenecks or challenges and solve them. Remember from earlier in this book that solving a problem for your customer should be your guiding principle. Are you staying true to that goal if you're hard to reach or not providing sufficient support to make your product or service useful?

---

5 http://www.forbes.com/sites/alexlawrence/2012/11/01/
   five-customer-retention-tips-for-entrepreneurs/

6 http://www.inc.com/geoffrey-james/customer-retention-keep-good-customers-from-
   leaving.html

Listen and engage

One of the challenges of providing great customer support is knowing what shortcomings you need to correct. In a not-too-distant past this was accomplished through surveys and focus groups. Today it's best accomplished by monitoring the social channels.

With all the chatter on social channels like Twitter and Facebook, there's a treasure trove of data to be mined that can help brands understand what your customers are saying. Social monitoring tools such as Radian6 and Wildfire can help you parse and understand social threats at an aggregate level.

It's not just about listening, though. Social channels also provide the opportunity for brands to answer back to their audience. This can be a profoundly useful tool to mitigate a crisis or to let your audience know they are being heard. Even better, you can proactively engage your audience for feedback on how to improve your services. Few things elicit loyalty more than a personal connection or a feeling that you helped shape the solutions offered by a company.

Customer outreach

Once you've made contact or established a relationship with a customer, you need to stay in touch with them. Unless you're one of the fortunate few who are uncontested leaders in your market segment, your customers and prospects are going to be regularly exposed to the brands of your competition, and the more time that passes since your most recent connection with them, the less likely you are to stand out as the first and best choice.

Consider what you can do to stay in touch with your customers and prospects. If you can get them to sign up for your newsletter, this gives you a direct opportunity to send offers and promote good news about your company. If you can get them to follow you on Facebook or Twitter, you can publish this same information to their newsfeed. If you have a more personal relationship with your clients, the same can be accomplished just by dropping them a note periodically. Let them know when you see an article or make a connection that would be meaningful to them.

Takeaways

- Traffic acquisition, conversion optimization, and customer retention have a compound effect. It's not enough to look at acquisition costs for a sale.

- Conversion goals and funnels can provide excellent opportunities for diagnosing bottlenecks in page flow.

- A/B testing is a method for serving variations of a page and measuring impact on a stated goal such as a purchase transaction. Changes in layout, marketing copy, colors, and images are common subjects for testing.

- Effective customer retention means not just reaching out to customers to keep those leads warm. It's also important to engage your customers and consider their feedback.

INDEX

ABOUT THE AUTHORS

Neal Cabage

Neal Cabage is a technologist and digital product strategist based in Los Angeles, California. He has consulted for companies like Macys.com, Disney, AIG, and a number of startups. He is a thought leader in online product strategy who has spoken at leading conferences on topics such as market discovery and data-driven conversion optimization.

Neal has successfully founded and sold two online startups, experiencing the full life cycle of a startup business, and spent years studying why online products succeed—all of which led to the development this book. Neal studied Music Technology at New York University and Psychology at the University of Washington, reflecting his interest in the intersection of technology and human experience.

Sonya Zhang, PhD

Sonya Zhang is a professor at the College of Business Administration, Cal Poly Pomona. She received her PhD in Information Systems and Technology from Claremont Graduate University, and holds a Master of Science in Computer Science as well as a Master of Business Administration. Sonya's research focuses on user experience, web and software development, analytics and optimization, and Internet entrepreneurship. She has published numerous articles in leading journals and conferences.

Prior to working in academia, Sonya was a software engineer in health informatics and higher education for over seven years. With her diverse academic background and industry experience, Sonya develops unique insights and expertise that bridge business and technology.

Learn more about the book and authors at http://TheSmarterStartup.com.

WATCH READ CREATE

Unlimited online access to all Peachpit, Adobe Press, Apple Training, and New Riders videos and books, as well as content from other leading publishers including: O'Reilly Media, Focal Press, Sams, Que, Total Training, John Wiley & Sons, Course Technology PTR, Class on Demand, VTC, and more.

No time commitment or contract required! Sign up for one month or a year.
All for $19.99 a month

SIGN UP TODAY
peachpit.com/creativeedge